The

Treasure

in the

Trauma

by Bobby Hannum

authorHOUSE®

AuthorHouse™
1663 Liberty Drive
Bloomington, IN 47403
www.authorhouse.com
Phone: 833-262-8899

Published by AuthorHouse 07/30/2024

ISBN: 979-8-8230-2396-2 (sc)
ISBN: 979-8-8230-2397-9 (e)

Library of Congress Control Number: 2024905314

Print information available on the last page.

A Tribute to my mentor in life (Daisaku Ikeda)

ˆIkeda Sensei (Daisaku Ikeda)

A few days ago, I received a message of the death of Daisaku Ikeda, who was 95 years old and passed away, November 15, 2023, of natural causes. After over fifty years of my Buddhist practice, I had come to take on Daisaku Ikeda as my mentor in life. That was not a decision made in haste. As an African American man born and raised in the southern United States, I most certainly was not seeking a Japanese man to take as my mentor in life. As a youth and a young musician on a quest for a much deeper understanding of life and someone who had such a history with health issues because of rheumatoid arthritis, I had a lot of motivation for staying with a movement that was mostly youth and had a great band and lots of opportunities to play with other musicians, when I joined this movement in Chicago in 1971. In any case, over the years, I watched this movement grow to be the largest Buddhist organization in the world, and the most diverse, as Soka Gakkai International, and it was clear to me that there was no one person who did more to make that happen than Daisaku Ikeda. After reading so many of his publications, there is no one I trust more than Ikeda Sensei in explaining the spiritual world in a scientific, realistic way. My story is not unique, I know other African Americans, Native Americans, and White Americans etc. that feel the same way.

Sensei!
Thank you so much, please rest in peace.

Acknowledgements

The first person I would like to acknowledge is my wife Mildred
for all her hours of solitude while I spent time trying to figure out
how to write and then the actual writing of this book. She also is the
person most responsible for my good health in my senior years due
to all the fresh vegetables I have consumed in the last forty years. To
her I express my deepest gratitude and that is still not enough.
Also, I would be remiss if I failed to acknowledge my mentor Daisaku Ikeda and all the SGI leaders who pushed me toward an understanding of the life I had been seeking in my darkest hours. And to
Guy McCloskey for his support toward the construction and editing
of this project.

In this book when I refere to WND-1 or WND-2, I am refering to,
The Writings of Nichiren Daishonin volume-1 and The Writings
Nichiren Daishonin volume-2

Preface

On more than one occasion while sharing my life experiences with a friend, I was told I should write a book, which I never really took seriously until I got older and realized that I have had some uniquely challenging experiences. Although, I have experienced many periods in my life that felt hopeless, I always felt there had to be a path to another moment of joy, even if it was just a moment. A real moment of joy doesn't have to last long, but once you experience it, it will always be something you will want to experience again. It was with that spirit that I was always determined to find my way out of the darkest moments of my life. When I seemed to be standing still and not moving, which at times was enticing, I felt like I was being swept away like a sick fish in a water stream. It was at those points I would realize that the important thing was to just keep moving forward. Finding my way through overcoming my health issues was my greatest motivation to keep moving forward. When I reached a point when doctors no longer had the answers I was seeking, I would be forced to seek elsewhere, if I were to keep moving forward.

It was through being exposed to hypnosis demonstrations, I started considering the powers of one's own mind more seriously. After searching a few religions on the concept of pray, I began approaching my health issues from within. Eventually, I began to solve all my problems from within, which led to my entire perception of my life and my environment. With that in mind, this is my story.

Table of contents

Chapter I Growing Up in Knoxville.................. 1
Early Memories.. 3
School Days 1... 5
Knoxville Children's Hospital..................................12
Aunt Edith & Aunt Kate..13
The Music in My Life 14
The Art in My Life..15
School Days 2 16
The Mouse...19
Awakening to the world of science 19
Returning to school... 20

Chapter II Chicago I............................. 29
Art Institute / Living in Hyde Park 31
Living in Woodlawn 36
Back to Hyde Park...38
The Dukorans.. 44
Working at Lying In.. 46
The "Party" 54
Black is beautiful, good hair/bad hair etc. 64
Leaving the High-Rise 65

Chapter III Chicago II............................ 83
NSA (Nichiren Shoshu of America)..................... 85
Harper Court... 88
Sucker and My Transitioning Into NSA................91
Suzanne... 94
The Youth Division Band....................................100
Lake Grove Chapter...102

Lorenzo's degeneration 105
Finding a Home for Ghanja..106
Tozan – My first pilgrimage 107
Barbara Julia Hannum 113
Rapid Circular Press... 114
Hyde Park District..119
BBJ..120
Supporting the Young Men 123
Hawaii Convention 125
Taking on Chapter level position and meeting Mildred..........126
Hyde Park Chapter 129
Knee Surgery 133
Dallas Convention 134
Veronica's Entrance..135

Chapter IV Phoenix, AZ 139

Our Apartment in Phoenix.. 141
Scott's Entrance..143
Family Ties in Phoenix 144
Imperial Lithographics..145
Phoenix Chapter..146
Mr. (Ted) Osaki 147
My Last Tozan (Pilgrimage) 148
April 11, 1991 149
Stories in Veronica's and Scott's early development 151
From NSA to SGI..152
R. A. Raises its Ugly Head..155
Gongyo and Daimoku 156
Leaving Imperial...157
Reviving my musical activity...158
AZ Performers Inc. 160
Minister of Ceremonies...160
Techniprint/AZ 162
An Awakening 163

Princess Tarrah Jewel...164
Red and Dad..165
The Last Year at Techniprint............................166
Whiskers & Oni..167

FNCC (Florida Nature and Culture Center)...........170

Chapter V The Way, I see It Now! 175

Mic and Mac / Does size ready matter?.................177
The Big Step! 178
The Ultimate Universe and the Ultimate Diety 180
The Three Treasures 183
The Ten Worlds 185
Three Thousand Realms in a Momentary State of Existence ...187
The Nine Consciousnesses.................................189
The Strict Law of "Cause and Effect"..................192
The Three Poisons..194
My Daily Practice 195
The Gohonzon..198
Mildred Today.. 202
The Clear Benefits of My Practice.......................203

I dedicate this book to
Veronica and Scott
(my daughter and son)
and
All the young people of the world

Chapter I
Growing Up
In
Knoxville

Early Memories:

My very first memory came when I was two years of age. It seemed to me that I literally walked into the life of Bobby Hannum as I was walking down some stairs and could hardly see because my eyelids were stuck together. As it turns out, according to adults involved at the time, I had 'caught a little cold' in my eyes. Whoever the adults in charge were, they put Vaseline on my eyes and took care of the matter almost immediately. My mother, my sister and I were temporarily staying at my aunt's house in the "projects" (a public housing community") called "Austin Homes" in Knoxville, TN., while we were transitioning into a house we were purchasing.

My very next memory was my third birthday. I remember getting a birthday card that, when I opened it, a big number "3" popped up. That happened after we had moved to 1333 Western Ave. After that my memories became more abundant.

I was born at 1308 Dora Street in Knoxville, TN., February 6, 1944. After spending my first two years there, my family, (my mother, father, sister, my maternal grandmother, and I) moved to the house where I grew up, which was 1333 Western Avenue. All this was in a neighborhood of Knoxville, called Mechanicsville, which is where I lived until I left Knoxville to go away to school. I remember being excited whenever my father, Robert Hannum Sr., would come home from his office as a dentist. We would always get hugs from him except for one night when, for some reason I had a screwdriver and I approached him in a threatening manner just for fun. He became very serious and let me know that that was not funny. It was a lesson I never forgot. During those days my job was to spend time with my mom. Mainly I would ride my tricycle around the house on a little walkway, which went all the way around our house and stayed within the boundaries of our property. Sometimes she would call me, and I would not come but instead run away around the house. I thought it was

3

very clever the way she would go around the other way and cut me off. For some reason I couldn't figure out how she knew to do that. Hetha was my older sister, born three years before me (1941) and Joy (my younger sister was born three years after me in 1947. 2 years after giving birth to my youngest sister, my mom gave birth to my younger brother, Stanford. However, we do have two half-sisters, Barbara, and Jewel, who were older than us from our father's previous marriage; and, a niece, Juan Zel, who was closer to the age of my youngest sister.

At this time throughout the United States, and particularly in the southern portion, everything was racially segregated. The earliest I remember experiencing racism personally was at five years old. My mother was teaching me how to cross the street. We lived on Western Avenue, a street that was quite busy even though it was only two lanes. She was sending me across the street for some reason to a little convenience store in a gas station. When I had crossed the street—which seemed like a very wide street to me—while she watched, a little white kid, not much older than me came up to me and grabbed me in a headlock. Of course, my mother, who was watching the whole time, came running over and started yelling at the kid. When the kid saw her, he ran off so quickly that he fell, then got up quickly and scampered off.

One day when I was six years old, without any warning to me, my mom called us together and told us that my father had passed away. I didn't know what "passed away" meant but, when they explained to me that I would never see him again, I cried. He had a heart attack after having smoked for many years. I guess I was too young, but I didn't cry at the funeral.

One of my favorite memories (although I'm not sure of the chronology of this event) was trying to have sex with the little girl next-door. I'm not sure how we knew what to do, although I suspect her older brother told us, but I'm not certain. I remember we were on either side of a wire fence with about four-inch squares between our houses and we were trying to do it through the fence.

We both seemed to know where things went but we just couldn't make it happen. After we figured out nothing was happening, we simply went about our business playing. As I started growing up considering that she was very blond, we were living in the south and I was black, I often wondered if they might lynch a 5-year-old for trying to have sex with a white girl. As it turns out that would be the closest, I would get to getting laid for the first 19 years of my life.

School Days 1

My school days begin at the age of five at Maynard Elementary School. It was quite a culture shock going from staying at home with my mom to hanging out with a lot of kids. You would think hanging out with those kids would sound like fun, but not for me. I cried every day for at least the first week. After that it wasn't much better. I had a difficult time in school and did not particularly like the other kids. Mrs. Tinsley was my first-grade teacher. She always wore a gray wig that looked a lot like the wig worn by the woman character played by Tony Perkins in the psycho movie, although the psycho movie had not come out yet. She was quiet a sweet old lady that had a good reputation and loved the kids.

I really didn't do very well in the first or second grade, maybe because I was five years old since my birthday was in February. So, I guess age-wise, I was a little behind the other kids. However, I started coming on strong in the third grade. By then I was enjoying copying material from the chalkboard. I also liked pulling the cute girls' hair, especially Jackie and Bonnie.

Now this was about the time for my short-term bullying stage. There was a kid my age--I think we were both small--and his name was Jack. Jack was relatively easy-going. However, every day after school I would harass him even with his two sisters around. I'm not sure where that mean streak came from, but it was something that I was never proud of. One day, when I was

5

hassling him, I realized someone had obviously taught him some skills. No matter what I would do he would get the best of me, and his two sisters who were still there, must have really enjoyed that. I, however, was crushed. I am sure when they got home, they had a lot to say to their family. I am so glad that happened to me early in life for that was the last time I was a bully.

This was about the time when Ronny moved in next door. Ronny and I turned out to be the best of friends. However, although we were next door neighbors, we could never go to school together because Ronny was white, and I was black and in Knoxville Tennessee at that time schools were still segregated. Everything was segregated to the point of having separate public bathrooms for Black people which of course were always substandard to the white ones. But when we were not in school, we were the best of friends. We did everything together. One time his mother or his aunt made us some superhero costumes that were matching. We would run around the neighborhood pretending to be superheroes. We would make clubhouses out of blankets or whatever was available. One time we made a clubhouse out of grass, which was one of our better clubhouses. However, whatever was in that grass was poisonous and we both broke out with red spots all over our skin.

Ronny was a bit of a daredevil. We used to ride piggyback on his scooter right down this hill into an intersection. I was never sure if we could have gotten out of the way if a car would have come, but nothing ever seemed to happen to him so I figured nothing would happen me either. A handyman once made a little car for me and my siblings with everything that a real car had, but without the engine, , and we would do the same thing with it, right down the hill into the intersection. We would be friends for years to come.

At the end of my block on Western Avenue which was to my left as I would come out of the front door of my house, there were a few small businesses which is about as far as I could go

6

without someone being with me. There was a small theater/movie house, a small grocery store and a shoe repair shop. I could go to the theater for $0.09 to see a movie and for the one cent I had left from a dime I could get a small pack of Kits, which was the small package of five taffy squares that came in different flavors. So, for one dime I could watch a movie and enjoy a pack of Kits. Of course, in those days you could buy a six-pack of soda pop for $0.25.

One day I was in the shoe shop for whatever reason while some kids were getting out of school. As close as I can remember I was about nine years old. Of course, this was a white school and one of the kids noticed me through the glass window in the shoe shop. He immediately let his other friends know that I was in the shoe shop, and I was not one of them, white. They begin waiting outside the shoe shop for me to come out. I knew that was exactly what I didn't want to do. So, I just stayed in there as long as I could. Soon they appeared to get interested in something else and left. When I saw the coast was clear, I came out and went home. However, for a little kid it was scary. I should mention that all the theaters were segregated and if it wasn't a black theater and you were black you would have to go upstairs and sit in the balcony. The fourth grade was pretty much uneventful. But the significance of the fourth grade was that it was my last year at Maynard Elementary School.

There was a new elementary school being built. It was called Cansler Elementary School. As it turned out, I was in the Cansler school district. Cansler was a newly built school and I enjoyed it a lot. Not only was everything new, but then there was Miss Brown. Miss Brown was young and had a great butt and was a great pianist, two qualities I liked a lot. She'd sometimes play the piano during our recess or while we were resting. She was my favorite teacher and I'm pretty sure I was her favorite student. One time she caught me running down the hall. She ordered me into the closet, where teachers were allowed to paddle the students' hand or bottom. She held my hand palm up and took the paddle and touched it as light as a feather and said, "Don't you do that again." I smiled and said I would not. During that class I never studied, and my spelling was terrible. I don't think I got two words correct the whole year. I also goofed off in other ways, so, she suggested that I may want to take the fifth grade a second time, and for me, that was a no-brainer. When my family found out that was my choice, they tried to discourage me from staying another year. However, I did stay back and enjoyed another year with Miss Brown. During the second year I studied all my spelling and missed no more than two words the whole year. It was during the second year with Miss Brown that I excelled most. I was at the head of my class in math and my only competition was a kid called Joseph who would go on to be the valedictorian when I graduated from high school. That year after being given a test I was told I had scored what was considered a tenth-grade level in English and had a very high level of mechanical perception, although I wasn't sure what that meant.

I think it was the summer at the end of the first year of the fifth grade that I got my first job with a paper route. It was a small African American newspaper by the name of "The Independent Call". I didn't do very well on the job. The little money that I would make, I would spend while I was on my route. And I was horrible at collecting the money. Of course, that job didn't last very long.

We were Seventh Day Adventists who attended church on Saturday. There was a deacon in the church who offered me a job in his piano shop remodeling pianos. Of course, I was simply a helper and he paid me minimally. There was an empty lot next door to the shop and whenever I wasn't busy, which was quite a bit of the time, I would play with the kids in that lot. We would have wrestling matches, throw horseshoes, and do lots of fun stuff. We would take old pianos, disassemble them, and take off all the old finish with a highly flammable material to refinish them.   One day I had made a match shooter, which was made from one of those old spring-loaded clothespins, which was popular at the time. The way it worked was, if you would put one of those wooden matches in it and pull the trigger, it would shoot out a flaming match. I discovered that shooting little drops of that flammable material, would produce these little explosions in a very cool manner. Even though I had been warned by the other kids, I continue shooting those little drops and soon that whole area was in flames. At this point I was panicking. I rushed inside to get a bucket and fill it full of water. I grabbed the bucket that was being used for garbage and I filled it full of water not realizing the bucket had a big hole in it. By the time I got to the fire, the water had leaked out and I threw a couple of cantaloupe rinds on the fire. Well, the fire department came out and put out the fire only after there was severe damage to the woodshed outside where we propped up the piano parts. After it was all over, I set there waiting to get fired. He came over to me and scolded me but to my amazement he did not fire me.

This is about when I started to develop personality traits that would last the rest of my life. I did enjoy my family. Wrestling with my younger sister and brother (Joy and Stanford). Hetha, my older sister, and I were, I think the closest, because we were there before the other two. But she always seemed to be doing her own thing because she was the oldest. It was about this time that we took a photo of the four of us for a Christmas card that even today when we get together, we try to emulate.

First Christmas card photo, Hetha, Bobby, Joy, and Stanford

Since we were Seventh Day Adventists, who worshiped on Saturday. Saturday was a big family day because all four of my mother's sisters would come over after church since my grandmother lived with us. We would always have a big meal on Saturdays when they came over. When we would have those family dinners, everyone would be very loud. When they were finished eating, they would find a bed in the house and take a nap. Then it was quiet.

After my father passed, Mama Dais (short for Daisy), my grandmother, took the role of housewife while my mother went to work. Mama Dais herself worked part time as a housekeeper / babysitter for a white family, a job that many black women her age held. She only had a third-grade level education, and I liked her straightforward answers to questions I would pose to her.

One such question was "if God made the earth, who made God." Her answer, without hesitation was "Oh! God has always been." She also did most of the cooking which included home-baked cakes, jelly, etc. She made a lot of canned food for the winter such as peaches and jellies. Twice a year she would clean the house immaculately, Christmas and spring.

Christmas was my favorite time of the year. Going caroling with the young people from our church, the way people were friendly to each other, the music, and the whole general spirit. In our living room, in which we were never allowed to play, there was a fireplace hidden behind a big easy chair. Only on Christmas Day would we move the chair and use the fireplace. Early in the morning the fireplace was started and around the Christmas tree we would open our gifts. Those were the days! In more recent years when Mildred, my wife, and I bought a house to raise our kids, it was essential (to me) that we have a fireplace. Every Christmas when our kids were growing up, I would get up early and light the fireplace for them to open their gifts.

I was a normal and active kid. I loved wrestling, but not so much boxing, I put on boxing gloves three times and lost definitively two out of three times. I didn't like those odds. I also had just joined the tryouts for a Little League baseball team and got a hit when I first stepped up to bat. It was just around this period my arms started aching badly. I think after a couple of times of that my mother took me to the doctor. And the doctor at that point diagnosed me with rheumatic fever. In the end, that would turn out to be a bad diagnosis. They immediately put me to bed for fear that I may have some heart issues. I don't remember how long I stayed in bed at that time, but it was long enough for my body to begin degenerating and getting very weak. I also don't remember ever attending school outside the home while I was in the sixth grade.

Knoxville Children's Hospital

It was around this time that I had two different stays in the Children's Hospital in Knoxville, for two weeks each. Believe it or not, on both occasions I really did enjoy it. The other children were fun despite their disabilities, and always seemed to display lots of energy, as kids do. Also, the personnel that worked there seemed to enjoy their jobs and spending time with the kids. The oldest kid that was there was about 19 years old, and he was a deaf mute. Since he was the oldest one there, he was sort of a Big Brother to everybody else. During my stay there he taught me the alphabet in sign language.

The most impressive kid there was Percy, (not his real name) who was five years old and a paraplegic. He was African American, full of life and more articulate than me and the other kids. Of course, everybody knew Percy and he was clearly the most popular kid there. He was there on both of my hospital stays and I assumed that he was staying there on a more indefinite basis. One time when I was there his mother came to visit him. I had never seen him so excited. He could hardly restrain himself. But when she had to leave, he cried. That was terribly moving. Remember, even though he spoke and act like an adult, he was only five years old.

There was what I think was the head nurse in the evening who I had a crush on. She had bright red hair and her name was June. She was playful and friendly with the kids. In the evenings I would ask her to page me as if I were a doctor. And with no hesitation she would page," Paging Dr. Hannum"," Paging Dr. Hannum." And I would get a real kick out of that.

At that time, I had no recognizable deformities that I was aware of. However, the experience at that hospital would prove to be very significant to me in coping with the health issues lying ahead in my life.

Aunt Edith & Aunt Kate

Aunt Edith was my father's sister and Aunt Kate was my mother's sister. Both were married and had no children, and they both reached out to my mother to lend support by offering to allow me to come and live with them, I guess to take the stress off my mother as a widowed mom at the time who was taking care of four kids. So, I first stayed with Aunt Edith.

Aunt Edith and Uncle Clarence lived on Mulvaney Street in Knoxville TN, right next door to the famous grandmother from the works of Nikki Giovanni, the great African American Poet. It is worth mentioning that my sister Hetha took her first piano lessons from Nikki's grandmother. What I liked most when I stayed at Aunt Edith's house was playing badminton across the street in the Cal Johnson Park. The park was very cool. After watching the adults play tennis, I would go over to the smaller badminton court and emulate them. Since I was doing it every day, I got very good at it. I rarely saw Uncle Clarence, who walked with an obvious limp, and I would only see him when he would come home from work late at night. I do remember Nikki Giovanni who was close to my age but had more interaction with my older sister Hetha.

Probably the most significant memory I have of the time I stayed at Aunt Edith's was the one time I offered a very strong prayer for a miracle to eliminate, my affliction of arthritis. When it didn't come, I was extremely disappointed.

When I stayed at Aunt Kate and Uncle Cecil's house it was sort of like Party City. They had a next-door neighbor who we called Aunt Sara, who really wasn't our aunt, but we called her that because she was so close to Aunt Kate. At one point when I was staying with Aunt Kate, Barbara, my oldest half-sister, was in town and was visiting Aunt Kate. Both Aunt Kate and Barbara, in my opinion, liked to party and they seemed to enjoy hanging out together. You see, Barbara was not that much younger than my mother and Aunt Kate. It was the last day before Barbara had to fly back to California where she was a schoolteacher. Uncle Cecil and I were sitting around, probably watching TV when Aunt Kate said with an almost child-like voice, "Barbara," I hope your plane flight, back home crashes." Abruptly, Uncle Cecil said, "Kate, what a horrible thing to say." And with that same child-like voice, she said, "Well I do." Barbara was so shocked she had to sit down. Saying that sort of thing was not so unusual for Aunt Kate since she drank quite a bit, and you never really knew what was going on in her head. Because of her drinking alcohol and smoking cigarettes, I thought Aunt Kate would die young, but of her four other sisters she was the last one to die. Although technically one of her older sisters did live a bit longer, they both died in their nineties.

The Music in My Life

This is probably a good time to address the early experiences I had with music. We always had an old upright piano in my house and at that time I guess having a piano in your home was quite common. I started experimenting on the piano at a very early age and figured out how to play simple melodies.

But, also at a very early age I acquired a ukulele. I had an uncle that showed me a few chords enough to get me started. When I got sick, a friend of mine from school named Timothy came by a few times to visit me. We were both small and very competitive in grammar school and he also played the guitar in his church, and he showed me some additional cords that got me on the path to being able to copy some popular tunes. At one point I got so proficient that my next-door neighbors, Ronny's parents, would ask me to perform Elvis Presley tunes for their family members. Now, as far as the piano was concerned, I always messed around with it, but my sister took piano lessons. My mother wouldn't allow me to take piano lessons because she was afraid that I would become gay. However, I did continue to try and at one point it seemed that suddenly I was able to play almost any tune

I tried to play. What had happened was that I discovered the three most fundamental cords of western culture music, the tonic, the dominant, and the subdominant, which were the first, fifth and fourth cords of the major/minor scale. When I was trying to play all those years, I became quite proficient at playing melodies with my right hand and by the time I was playing chords with the other hand I could play a lot of songs completely. I was raised as a Seventh Day Adventist, and I also had some experience as a young kid singing in the church children's choir. We also formed a quartet with three other youth in the church as we got a little bit older.

It was about this time that I came into possession of a marching snare drum. It seems that I was planning on using it when I transitioned to the seventh grade of junior high school. At that point I begin playing the drum to music on the radio, which at that time was mostly Rock and Roll. I will say that I noticed it was incredibly easy for me to follow any rhythmic pattern I heard on the radio, along with all the varied rhythmic accents.

The Art in My Life

During the period when I was home by myself quite a lot, was also the period when I discovered my ability to draw and paint. I would draw faces and landscapes and the adults in my life would encourage me to consider pursuing art. After looking at my drawings and paintings, my mother decided to enroll me in a correspondence art course at the Minneapolis Art Institute in Minneapolis MN., which I completed.

That would later be my motivation for studying art in high school.

Painting from age 12

15

School Days 2

Okay, here I was, restricted only to bed rest. Of course, I still had to get an education, so the school had to come to me. I had what they called a homebound teacher. She did not come every day, so I had a lot of days by myself that would prove to be quite a challenge. I watched a lot of television, particularly old romantic movies. In the evenings after everyone else got out of school and off work, sometimes Ronny would come over and shoot marbles with me. Most of the time I think he just let me win because of his compassion. During the day when no one was there I developed games. Since I was lying in the bed a lot, sometimes I was dozing off, in and out of a sleep state. I had such a desire to go outside that I would pretend that I was floating out of my body and between our house and the one next door. During that period, I had developed the ability to wake up in the middle of a dream, go to the bathroom and then come back and resume the dream where I left off. That was particularly good when I was not ready to finish the dream.

I would also dream a lot about my ability to fly. Although, my flying was not like the flying of Superman, I could float and get higher and higher. However, many times I did try to fly like Superman, but I just could never go fast enough. Because my dreams and my reality became so close, I was beginning to think that I could really fly. In my dreams I could stand up and lift one leg off the ground and then lift the other one off the ground. It was so real I just thought I could probably do that. Sometimes that method of entertainment got a little scary. For example, if the phone rang, I would sit up to go answer it but many times I realized that I was just dreaming that I was sitting up and sometimes I would panic and didn't know if I was sitting up or dreaming that I was sitting up. And by getting so paranoid it made me unsure of myself in a possible emergency. At some point I even thought I saw shadows at the door and was really freaking out when I was unable to sit up.

Later in life as I was reading about astral projection it seemed to me that I was experiencing some of the same things they addressed. Also, about that time I began to have frequent nightmares. I think one of my aunts told me if I slept with a Bible under my pillow they would go away. So, I did, and they did go away, although I will say that I attributed it to the power of suggestion more than an intervention from God. However, at the time, whatever worked was fine with me.

A short time later I had a surprise birthday party which I believe was my 12th birthday, which would mean that I was in the second half of my seventh-grade year, but at this time I was still not back in school. It was quite a surprise. It was the first time that I experienced tears that were not caused by sadness. Except for Ronny, my next-door neighbor, I think everyone else were family members. The only problem with that is that it was a little bit sad that I was unable to have a birthday party with friends my age. I guess I was mostly moved by my family caring enough to cheer me up. That was moving.

This was about the time the doctors caring for me decided that they had done everything they could do. I often wondered would they have tried more if I were white. Well, my mother had no other choice but to consult our family doctor. Although some accused him of drinking heavily, he carried on his practice respectably and he was able to help me considerably. At some point they figured out that instead of having rheumatic fever I had rheumatoid arthritis.

I was visiting Dr. Williams' office when I experienced what I felt was the most emotionally traumatic moment of my young life. His office was in a populated area and the time that I visited him was the time when the schools were letting out. I was coming down the stairs at the doctor's office very weak and could hardly stand up, feeling like a very old man and my legs were wobbling. At that point many of the kids I used to go to school with saw me coming down the stairs and I felt totally exposed. My young ego was crushed. There are no words to describe the emotional pain I experienced at that moment.

After a while with the care of Dr. Williams I was able to try to go back to school. I started attending Beardsley Junior High. At this point I had what I call my very first girlfriend. Keep in mind at this point in my life to have a girlfriend meant that you told everybody you were boyfriend and girlfriend, and you would carry her books home after school. That's about as far as I got in my romantic life. Her name was Lovie (I know that's hard to believe) and she was very cute, and I think she was one of the most popular girls in that grade. Now you're probably thinking this puny little kid came back to school after being sick and landed a girlfriend like this.

At this point I must bring up a phenomenon in the African American community that was way bigger than I was. You see the only thing that I had going on was that I was light skin, and it sadly gave me an edge. The people who had straighter hair were considered to have good hair. This is a situation that people in the black community still may not be completely free of today, I think this was what I refer to as a "slave or underdog mentality," but I can discuss that later. Girls would literally flirt with me on the way to school. One time I even got into a scuffle about Lovie in the gymnasium with the kid who probably understood that I did not deserve her. In any case I didn't stay in school very long before I was homebound again, so actually my romance was over. I learned later that she became pregnant by a 19-year-old kid.

Being homebound was not always that bad. One day my teacher who walked on crutches because of polio, I think, brought with her a student who was about my age, but she was adorable. Apparently, she had some illness that required her to be home-instructed. All I can say is she looked perfect to me, and it was sad to think that she did have an illness that serious. I only saw her a couple or three times. The last time I saw her, we were in high

18

school, and it was some related gathering of students who had been home instructed. She was so sweet and had such a great personality and I often wondered what happened her.

The Mouse

There is one event that I would like to bring up that happened around this time. Air rifles or as we used to call them BB guns, were quite popular at the time. Of course, I always wanted one but like many parents, my mother was reluctant to get me one. It reminded me of the movie that came later where the kid wanted a BB gun, but everyone kept telling him, "You'll shoot your eye out." Well, that sounded exactly like my mother. However, at that time I think my mother was feeling sorry for me and broke down and bought a Daisy Cub air rifle for me. At one point I saw a mouse under the water heater in the kitchen. To catch that mouse, I put a piece of cheese right where I had seen the mouse. I then set up a chair with my BB gun and waited for the mouse to come and grab the cheese. This is where it got interesting. The mouse did not come out. That is, until I forgot about him and then when I look back the cheese was gone. That happened more than once. And then I begin to think, "How is he doing that?"

Then I remembered the game we used to play where you would stare at someone until they turned and looked at you. I played that game so many times, I became convinced that some sort of telepathy was going on. I reasoned that the mouse must have been feeling my intensity to kill him. After all, for that mouse the situation was life or death. Based on that, I've always sort of believed we had some mental connection with each other, including animals. I never was able to get that mouse.

Awakening to the world of science

It was at this stage in my life when I met Mr. Cooper. Mr. Cooper was a friend of my mom and would visit us frequently. He was a physics teacher at Knoxville College, the local Black college. While talking to him I discovered the wonders of physics and how it applied to life. Once he even took me to his classroom and showed me around. After listening to his explanation of things, he would pose questions to me about how the physics of things worked. I was encouraged by the interest he took in me, and it opened in me an interest in science that would last for the rest of my life.

Prior to Mr. Cooper, the only thing I knew about the history of the world as a planet was whatever I learned in church. To me the world of physics and science made so much more sense in explaining life. What was interesting to me was the fact that Mr. Cooper belonged to the same church that I attended. I never understood how he could believe in the physics that he demonstrated to me and the doctrine that was taught in the church. One of my greatest regrets is the fact that I was never able to share my Buddhist teachings with Mr. Cooper before he passed away. For me, Buddhism is the only major religion that uses the concepts of faith in prayer without contradicting science in any way. However, today with quantum physics things are changing for the better.

Returning to school

After the eighth grade, while under homebound care, Dr. Williams decided that I had improved enough to try to go back to school. I think I was in the ninth grade and when I returned to school things were very different. I did not seem to have the appeal with the ladies that I had when I was in the seventh grade. All the guys had gotten bigger, stronger and the popular guys were playing with school sports teams. At this point I was pretty much an observer, it appeared. I did decide to join the band as a drummer, which seemed to come very easy to me.

About this time while I was just trying to cope with being back in school a strange thing happened. When the teacher would ask me questions in class, I would just try to answer them in a polite and sincere way. But I noticed as I was explaining things the kids would laugh, but not like they were making fun of me. They thought the way I expressed myself was very humorous. It appears they thought I was being facetious. So, I thought this didn't feel too bad, so, why fight it. Suddenly, I was the class clown, which gave me new popularity. Somewhere down the line because I was so small, I acquired the nickname, Herc, short for Hercules, which I willingly embraced.

Beardsley Junior High was grades 7 through 10. After that I would be going to Austin High, the only Black high school in Knoxville, Tennessee at the time. Nothing spectacular happened to me between the 9th and 10th grades at Beardsley. Although there was one wrestling match I saw when I was walking down one of the halls that was very impressive. It was two small guys that were pushing each other for a reputation; one was Sammy and the other one was the younger brother of a friend of mine called Eddie. I think Eddie and his younger brother had a father that taught them some self-defense skills.

I'm not sure where Sammy got the skills, but he had plenty of them. He and I worked at a party one time when we both were dressed up in Turkish costumes and would light cigarettes and do whatever necessary to make the guests more comfortable. It should be noted that all the guests were white, and Sammy and I were African American. So, I guess you could say I was closer to him. In any case it was very impressive the way they moved around; it was very fast-moving, one move after the other and it lasted for about a good two minutes. It ended by Eddie's younger brother grabbing Sammy by the collar, putting his foot in Sammy's stomach, and throwing him backwards over his head. While Sammy was in the air, he rotated his body around and came down on top of the head of Eddie's younger brother--an incredible move-- and when he landed on the floor, he pinned Eddie's younger brother down simultaneously.

Eddie's younger brother challenged me one time in the hall, maybe because I was also small, but I knew I was not in their league. I declined. However, when I was a senior in high school, a kid did challenge me in the hall and I felt confident since he was young and little bit chubby that I could take him down in a few seconds, and that's exactly what happened. I guess, understandably, I looked like a pushover. I guess you could say my health had improved a bit by then.

After Beardsley came Austin High School. The first day I entered Austin was for orientation. I remember walking into the auditorium that was already full of students. As I walked into the door, I noticed a row of young men. The one at the end of one row punched the one next to him on the shoulder. And the one he had punched turned and punched the guy next to him on the shoulder and the chain reaction of punching the guy next to you on the shoulder began. About midway across the row a switchblade flashed and ended the chain reaction. At that point everyone laughed enthusiastically. That was the first thing I saw when I entered Austin High School, and it made a big impression on me.

I think Austin was the place I first met Ernest. Ernest and I both had a slightly deformed right hand; his was from a car hood slamming down on his wrist and mine from the Rheumatoid Arthritis. He became my Number One partner as the class clown team. I think it was the chemistry class where we were most active. Along with being partners in crime in the classroom, we also use to play bongos together. We played at a couple of events such as pep rallies. One such event was in the auditorium where we played and I did the twist, a popular dance at the time. My mother was there and was surprised when the kids cheered me on in my dance segment. She later expressed to me that she had no idea I was so outgoing. Those pep rallies were my first experience of being cheered by an audience, although I did have a little experience in the classroom. At that point I was ready to be a performer.

About halfway through the year, the teacher began to come

into the class and say, "Robert Hannum and Earnest Long go to the library" before he said anything else, because he had no patience to deal with us that day. It was also in that class that something horrible happened. We were experimenting with phosphorus, and we had to burn the spoons that we used thoroughly when we finished. I burned the spoon that I had until it was red, then white-hot, as we had been instructed to do. When I finished, I took it over to the teacher and asked him was the spoon burned out sufficiently. He wasn't really paying attention to what was happening, and he reached out and grabbed the spoon. And everybody in the class laughed. At this point the teacher thought I did that as a joke. He reported the incident, and I was expelled from school. However, my mother came down to the school and after a long conversation I was allowed to come back to school. He never knew it was truly an accident. I would never have done something that cruel.

While I was in high school, I worked as a janitor in a small insurance company where my mother had worked previously. When I was healthy enough my mother always saw to it that I had a job. This office was in a small area that was simply called "The Corner". The Corner was an intersection of College and University. Knoxville College, the only black college in Knoxville, was located on College Street and I'm not sure if University Ave. had any connection with University of Tennessee, which was not too far away. However, the only education you might get on The Corner was that of nightlife. It was a popular area with Black folk who were into the nightlife. There were three pool halls on The Corner, which my mother considered sinful places. Of course, I thought they were very cool places.

I started hanging out in one of the pool halls, even though I was underage. I even looked younger than I really was, but nobody seemed to care, except my mother. Once just after school, Leroy (a kid I grew up with) got beaten up pretty badly right outside that pool hall by a kid we went to school with whose name escapes me, so I'll call him JT. JT was a skinny kid who was well dressed, full of confidence and popular with the girls. Leroy was muscular, and I suspect underestimated JT. One day while we were playing pool, JT pretended to attack me and flipped me up-side-down so fast that my feet hit the ceiling and then I landed on my feet. When that had happened, I thought, "Wow, JT is nobody to fuck with!"

I would hurry and finish my work at my job so I could go hang out at the pool hall and act cool and grown-up. That is up until the time when my mother was looking for me and my little brother, Stanford, proceeded directly to the pool hall, stuck his head in the door and said "Bobby, Mama is looking for you." That was embarrassing, and I had to take a little break from the pool hall. I didn't return until I graduated and left town. There was a saying around there, "If you want to be successful you must first graduate from The Corner. Many people didn't. After I left town to go to school and during my first visit back home, I went to that pool hall. I was welcomed warmly. I guess I had graduated from The Corner.

Let me not forget my knife-slinger period. I was influenced by the experience I had when I first walked into the school when kids that were punching each other stopped abruptly when a kid displayed a knife. Of course, I thought that was very cool. I had two knifes, one was a hooked knife like the ones that were used for cutting carpet and the other like a long straight blade, and they both folded back into the handle. I practiced a lot in front of a mirror until I was able to get the knife out of my pocket to a visible defensive position in one fluid motion with no extra movement to open the blade. One would just see the blade and hear the click of the blade opening in an instant.

The first time I pulled it out in school was when we're goofing around, and one kid was playfully attacking me. When I pulled it out, the other kids were extremely impressed. They were giving each other high fives etc. as if they had seen a killer dunk in a game of hoops. The other kids would frequently pretend to attack me so they could see me draw my knife. I was getting quite a reputation. Then one day when I was standing in the hall, a kid who I had never seen before, approached me in the hall and said "I heard you were quick with your knife. Do you think you're faster than me? I looked at him for a second or two and then walked away. I didn't like where that seemed to be going. That was the beginning of the end of my knife slinger days. After all I knew what I was: I was a "not so tough kid" surviving in a tough kid's world.

And then there was Saundra. She had long hair, long legs and was quite popular with all the guys. Of course, I, like all the other guys was all eyes for Saundra. I think in my senior year, I was taking what I think was a history class with Saundra. We used to talk with each other so much that the teacher decided to put us at a table next to his desk so he could keep an eye on us. I was facing the class, and she was facing me, sharing a slightly larger desk between us. As far as the two of us hooking up was concerned, Saundra really was way out of my league. She had a boyfriend that was older than all of us and he had a reputation for knocking people out. We still talked a lot and our talking evolved into games under the table. She used to tease me by opening her legs under the table and I would put my leg as far between her thighs as I could. Saundra, wherever you are, thank you for the most fun I had in high school.

The most significant thing that happened to me in my senior year was Mr. Winton and Art class. Austin High was also a vocational school and there were things like Auto Mechanics, Commercial Cooking and Commercial Art, etc. available. I think I had begun taking some interest in my junior year when I discovered the Commercial Art's class. I had taken an art correspondence course when I was about 12 and did quite a bit of drawing and painting that I was encouraged to do by an artist friend of my family. Mr. Winton who was very aware of my reputation, was very reluctant to let me in his class. After he saw my artwork, he decided to give me a chance. So, in my senior year I took his art class for what I think was three hours a day. Then if I remember correctly, the other three hours were academics.

After he saw that I was serious, he suggested that I go to art school and he said that there was no better art school than his alma mater, the Art Institute of Chicago. He told me that Eddie, who was his best art student and one year ahead of me, was going to the Art Institute of Chicago. He was very proud of having gone to the Art Institute and he was trying to spark my interest. Then he showed me their catalogue. As I thumbed through it, I saw a classroom with a nude woman posing in front of the class. Then I asked Mr. Winton, "Do they have nude models in the class-room?" He said, "Yes". I said, "Okay I'm in." After all, I could think of worse ways to spend time in the classroom than drawing naked women and not getting in trouble for it. So, Mr. Winton went to work with my mother, and I guess the school authorities and somehow an organization that helped rehabilitate kids with special needs (God knows I had special needs) came up with 4a four-year scholarship to the Art Institute of Chicago.

As the school year was ending, there were traditional activities such as the prom and class trip. I did not attend the prom, but I sort of wished I had gone after I heard that there was a big brawl there with a lot of damaged white coats. That would have been fun to watch (from a distance). I did go on the class trip, and it was a bit underwhelming. I bought a cold can of beer and my favorite hamburger from a popular restaurant across the street from the school, of course, forgetting that when I reached our destination, the beer would be warm and the hamburger cold. We went to a lake of some sort that I don't remember much about, but the couples seemed to be having the most fun.

Another activity I had was certainly the wildest one I had experienced at the time. Whatever the purpose for this activity was, it amounted to going out and partying with some of my other classmates. A couple of my friends had been allowed to take their parents' cars and we were free to go where we wanted to. We decided to go to Lonsdale. Of all the black communities in Knoxville TN, Lonsdale was considered the toughest, (at least in the circles I ran in). Although I went to school with many kids from Lonsdale, I had never spent much time there. On the way there of course, we raced the cars. The friend that I was riding with was Hubert and the other friend was Leroy. Hubert was driving a "54 Chevy and Leroy was driving a '62 Ford. We were amazed to discover that the '54 Chevy was faster than the '62 ford.

In any event we went to this nightclub in Lonsdale. I saw many of my friends there, which was comforting. I had never done any serious drinking, at least until that night. I got plenty loaded. I proceeded to make an ass of myself in many ways, most of which I don't really remember. But there was one incident that I remember very well. I was going to the bathroom and when I got to the door, I kicked open the door, slamming it against the wall. And who was standing there taking a leak? Dog, who was considered the meanest, toughest guy of our generation in Lonsdale, and already had a reputation for killing a man. He turned to me and said, "Man, do you know who I am"? Well, right then I knew I was in trouble, but I was too drunk to stop myself. Then I replied, "Dog or something like that". By then the door had closed and I was standing there for what seemed a long time when, abruptly the door swung open and a couple of friends of mine who happened to live in Lonsdale, rushed in and grabbed me and said to Dog, "Dog he's just drunk and don't know what he's doing".

I was so drunk I wasn't sure who to thank for possibly saving my life. I think one may have been "Sweet Baby" the younger of two brothers ("Sweet Baby" and "Baby Brother"). But I'm not sure. Both of whom were considered ladies' men. Anyway, let's talk a little bit about Dog. When I was a kid about 7 or 8 years old, our church took us around to comfort those who were "less fortunate" than we were. Although I think our presence probably made them feel uncomfortable. We were visiting an orphanage when I first saw Dog. He was a kid maybe a year older than I was. I don't think our eyes ever made contact, but he sure made an impression on me. A little later in the fourth grade I saw him in my class. I don't think I ever had a conversation with him. As we grew older, I saw him rarely. The last I heard was that he passed away on the streets of a big city up north like Chicago or Detroit. I hope that wasn't true. Of course, that wasn't his name and I think I do remember it, but I will leave it unsaid. Oh, how my heart goes out for that brother.

Well, the school year was over, and I must prepare for my future in Chicago. Mr. Winton took me under his wings. He decided to take me to Chicago the summer before I started school. I think we must have registered while we were there. He was my first experience that I had with a true mentor and unfortunately, I didn't understand or appreciate it. I guess this was about the time when the reality of being on my own set in. It was a scary feeling but the anticipation of what lies ahead was much stronger. Chicago, here I come!

Chapter II
Chicago I

Art Institute / Living in Hyde Park

I don't really remember the trip to Chicago, but my mother had planned for me to stay with a friend of hers while I was attending school. Sammy, her friend, owned a big mansion-type home in Hyde Park, which was a very wealthy area in its heyday. When I moved in, there were two other boarders, Cliff, and Lionel. There was also a housekeeper named Jacob who I think stayed with the house from the last owner and lived in the basement. Cliff was an ex-boxer who was now a schoolteacher in the public school system. Lionel was a student who had been living in Montreal, Canada, but was originally from Barbados. He was a tall good-looking guy with a Barbados accent who women were always hitting on. Jacob was openly gay, but not flaming in his appearance. I was given a small room on the second floor, where I could play my little cheap transistor radio without disturbing anyone.

When I started attending classes at the Art Institute, I suddenly realized what an impressive place it was. In the back of this huge building was the school. Behind the building were patios and beyond that was Lake Michigan. On the north end of the building was Goodman Theater, an acting school where the likes of Marlon Brando had attended. The most spectacular thing was the huge museum in the front of the building with original works of all the old masters: da Vinci, Rembrandt, Picasso, Van Gogh, and the list goes on. The curriculum consisted of basic classes such as painting, drawing 2d and 3d design, some exposure to sculpting, ceramics, photography etc. It was actually a very exciting place to go to school.

I'm not sure exactly when I started working, but it wasn't long before I had a job at a fast-food restaurant called The Cow. The Cow was known for their fries that were thin-sliced potatoes that were sliced on the spot and deep-fried. It was located just a few blocks from where I lived. Hyde Park was a very cool place to live. It was a community surrounding the University of Chicago and many of the businesses catered to the students. Next to The Cow was a bookstore called the Green Door. In the rear of the Green Door was a coffee shop called The Medici. The clientele for all three places were both students from nearby University of Chicago and neighborhood teens. So, at the age of eighteen it was a fun place to work.

Since I was attending school during the day, I was hired for the evening shift. After I had been trained, I was the only one staffing the place in the evenings. As far as I can remember the menu consisted of hamburgers, hot dogs, soft drinks, milk shakes and of course "cow fries." I would take over in the afternoon and close about 10:00 or 11:00 pm, clean up and finish about midnight. When that routine went on for a while, I started enjoying what I called my thinking period. I guess my most exciting moment was when I concluded that something in life was eternal. I'm sure it was a result of the conversation I had with my grandmother when I was a little kid, about where God came from. I wasn't too certain about the existence of God, but I did pray every night, asking "If you are there, please show me some proof." I think that those prayers were the last prayers I had as a Christian, although I do think that prayer was answered.

I only went to the Art Institute for one year but of those people I hung out with, four became a part of my life after I left. Those were Gina, Denver, Lorenzo, and Fee; all of whom were African American, with Gina being the exception. Lorenzo, I first remember playing bongos in the cafeteria. Since I had played bongos in high school, he struck a chord with me right away. When I first played with Lorenzo there was a definite familiarity when I would look over my shoulder and see these long slender fingers slapping the bongos. It was almost like Ernest was there. Then somehow Fee showed up with some bongos. The three of us formed an immediate friendship. I think Denver joined us later when we were transitioning to the larger, conga drums.

There were quite a few good-looking girls in that freshman

class and Gina was one of them. Many of them appeared to me to be a little snobby. But Gina was not one of those. There were also two other students that were also friendly. Pat, an African American especially might account for why she wasn't snobby, and the other one was Hungarian who had a lot of Black musician friends and was just a cool human being. The Hungarian's name was Buffy who was also my neighbor and I babysat for her roommate's daughter a few times. These were the people that I seemed to migrate toward throughout that school year. In April of that school year, I think a teacher had suggested we could go to the Natural History Museum and do some sketching of the prehistoric animals. There were at least three of us who said we would be there: Gina, Pat, and myself.

As it turns out the Sunday, we were supposed to meet was Easter Sunday. However only Gina and I showed up. I'm sure because it was Easter, we both had dressed up for the occasion. When I saw her walking toward me with her hair loose and freshly done, I thought, "Damn, I think I'm in love." At the time her hair was long, and she obviously had a little more curl in her hair than normal. I don't remember doing one sketch. We decided to go to my place in Hyde Park. When we got outside, we were walking, the wind was blowing and her hair blew in my face, and I felt a déjà vu moment. I told her about it, and then I said "Gina, I think you're my dream girl." We both laughed and then we took the Illinois Central commuter train and proceeded to my place in Hyde Park. By this time, I had moved out of the little room into a two-room suite with nice sized rooms. I did not make any real physical advances toward her, although our interest in each other was very clear. Needless, to say, our relationship developed into a most wonderful romance.

Gina lived in a suburb of Chicago. Her parents were probably in the category of blue-collar community and were not parents (particularly her father), who could welcome their daughter's black boyfriend into their home, which was the case with most white America at the time. Although her father was German and her mother was Italian, Gina was Italian thru and thru. She loved talking about her Italian relatives and loved to cook the Italian dishes she learned from her mother. When we wanted to be together, she would have to take the train to Hyde Park in Chicago and then back home before it got too late. Sometimes it was too late and too dark, and I worried about her.

We did have a social life involving other people, which is certainly healthy for a young couple. We went to a few parties. Guys were always hitting on her, and I got the distinct feeling that they couldn't see why she was with me. Sometimes I felt the same way. One of my favorite times of our early dates was the time we went on a double date with Plato Jones and his girlfriend. I had just met Plato and he liked hanging out and playing conga drums with Lorenzo and me. He was very outgoing and well-liked by the ladies. I think he moved away to Arizona with his parents, but I heard he had been playing congas with some famous groups. In any case it was a fun date with Plato, throwing firecrackers all over the place like a little kid and us winding up in the back room of some party making out with our girlfriends. At this stage of my life my health was better than it had been in a long time. I had even been working out a bit with Cliff, the ex-boxer, who was also on a track team that trained at the University of Chicago campus. I remember hanging out with a few guys including Plato and Fee (I think) at what I think was Fee's place, because the only woman there was Fee's wife, Margie. We had had a couple of little scrimmages, and I was feeling confident. After talking a little shit, Fee and I squared off in what was the more intense battle. While we were going at it, I remember hearing Margie saying "Bobby's fast" as if she was surprised. That reminded me of when I was a kid and other kids cheering wrestlers on. The more they cheered for you the stronger you felt. I was feeling in control when suddenly Fee gave a big thrust, and I went sliding across the floor. After pausing for a couple of seconds, everyone burst out in laughter. Well, I was outweighed by at least 20 pounds and there is nothing more unforgiving in a wrestling match than being too lightweight. But that was so much fun, and I felt like a kid again and it was such a joy to feel that after those years of being laid up.

At age 18 all young men had to report to the draft, which I had done. Now I was 19 and I received a letter from the US Selective Service System telling me to report for active duty. The wording of the letter led me to believe that if I didn't show up on time (about 7am) for the physical I would automatically be enlisted and shipped out.

I was so afraid that I set two alarm clocks the night before; one was next to my bed and the other was across the room on a dresser. I guess I was hard to wake up because when I woke up the next morning the clock next to the bed was turned off and the one that had been across the room was under my pillow. I was panicking. On my way there I imagined having to fight with those rifled bayonets. Those things looked heavy, and I couldn't imagine fighting someone with one. When I got there, I gave them my papers, fully expecting them to say, "Oh you're late, go get in the line that gets shipped out today." But what they said was" Follow the red line.". As it turns out, once they examined the nodules on my right and left elbow, they gave me a "4F" rating. Okay, call me Chicken Shit, but I was relieved. I guess they couldn't see me out there fighting with bayonets either.

During this period, I had come across a fife, a little flute-like instrument which I became quite proficient with in a fairly short time. A little later while I was visiting friends or family of Fee's I ran into an old wooden flute with metal keys. Noticing that basically it was the same as the fife, I picked it up and started playing it. The people who I was visiting said that since I seemed to be the first person to make a decent sound with the flute, that I should take it. After a while I got a traditional metal flute that eventually led me to music school.

Fee and his wife, Margie, were an interracial couple. Since Fee had gone to school with Gina and me, it was easy to see why Fee and Margie became our first friends as a couple.

Since that Easter when Gina and I truly discovered each other, my passion for school dwindled big time. I was way more interested In Gina than I was art. Spring was here and for me the Art Institute and its beautiful surroundings had become just a background for our romance. It seemed like most of the time we were out on the patios by the lake making out. Yep, I had it bad. I struggle with the time and the chronology of it all, but it seemed that about this time I lost my job at The Cow. One day the owners just came in and shut it down. The school had connections to jobs in the community to help students make extra money. I took advantage of this resource and began working at Washington Photo Engraving.

Living in Woodlawn

Maybe it was because it became clear that I was not going back to the Art Institute, but at some point, Sammy told me it was time to find my own place. So, I found a room in Woodlawn, which was a major step down from Hyde Park. To get an idea of the area I watched from my window, a gathering of about 100 young Black men/boys declaring themselves what turned out to be the Blackstone Rangers, which was considered by some one of the most notorious young street gangs in the country at that time. It was a far cry from the cushy two-room suite at Sammy's house. I remember one week when my weekly pay was approximately $12.80, and my weekly rent was $12.50, so that was a difficult time. It was at this point that I smoked my first joint, which would be the beginning of a long-term relationship.

Gina was incredible. Her support was above and beyond anything I could have expected. She would visit me at my job, sometimes maybe bring a sandwich or help me if I had no pocket change and come visit at my place. She eventually moved in with me. Woodlawn could be a scary place at times, especially for a young white girl. Fee and Margie also had an apartment in Woodlawn. Gina and I spent at least a few nights with them waking up in the morning to a Lou Rawls album, which I think Fee had rigged up as our alarm clock. I remember one hot muggy night when we had to walk from their apartment to ours, when we stepped outside onto the sidewalk the most intense feeling came over me. It was like an angry human spirit was in the air. During that walk of about five blocks, we saw, I think, about two maybe three altercations and one woman that seemed intoxicated jumped out of a dark doorway and yelled to Gina, "white bitch". We did get home safely but that very intense feeling in the air, was an experience I will never forget, and I have only experienced it to that extent twice in my life. I will address the second time a little latter.

Another time when Gina and I were walking down the street, a pebble hit my shoulder from behind and when I turned around about three or four guys behind us were grinning. I then took her hand and turned back forward, and a voice said, "You better hold her hand." The worst thing that happened was when Gina was coming home after dark, and some guy tried to snatch her purse. She started yelling, which was good, but she wouldn't give up her purse, which was bad. Apparently, some of our neighbors heard her and yelled out of the window to the assailant and he ran off, although he did punch her attempting to get the purse. When I came home, she told me the story but seemed to be physically ok. I thought many times that she could have been home in the suburbs having a reasonably peaceful existence, but instead she was there in that hellhole with me and never showed the slightest evidence of discontentment.

My goal was to get out of Woodlawn, but we also wanted to get married. I wanted to get married, but I also wanted to live long enough to get married. In that environment that wasn't certain. Maybe I blocked a lot of those memories out of my mind, but it seems that we were not there that long. However, we had to have been there a while, we waited until I was twenty-one for us to get married.

Our getting married was not just a slam-dunk. As I said before, I was bought up as a Seventh Day Adventist. The Adventist Church was racially segregated at the time. Somehow Gina had acquired some white Adventist friends, who had begun putting pressure on her about marrying a Black man. Her friends then suggested that she should visit their minister. In my heart I didn't care what the white minister thought, but we agreed to go, and we took with us Sammy who was black, an educator and a deacon in the Adventist Church. My real goal was to point out the absurdity of the racism in the church. In the end the white minister seemed to admit that that was a racist view, but he said, "I have seen some things". I guess "some things" that would justify his racism.

Well, it did all work out, and we got married a few days after my birthday. The wedding was a small ceremony in Sammy's house with a minister I had as a child in Knoxville. Of course, my mother flew in for the ceremony. During the actual ceremony I was extremely nervous. I was so nervous that my right knee started to buckle, and Gina had to physically support me. I never really understood why I was so nervous. After the wedding, I don't really know how long we stayed in Woodlawn, but it seemed that shortly after that I took on a slightly better job at a place called Liberty Photo Engraving and we moved into a high-rise apartment in Hyde Park.

Back to Hyde Park

I really liked Hyde Park. It was a very cool place to live. In Hyde Park there were plenty of interracial couples and no one really noticed us. That's not to say that it was free of racism. When we were looking for an apartment, there were plenty of places that very outwardly said they didn't rent to colored people.

Although by this time the Civil Rights Act was already in place, I guess it took a while to take effect. I think by this time Gina had landed a job as Museum Secretary of the Oriental Institute at the University of Chicago. Contrary to its name it was an archaeological museum that seemed to me to deal with ancient Egypt and the surrounding areas. Because Gina was employed by the University of Chicago, there was housing that was made available to faculty and staff. I think it was through that channel that we found that apartment. It was a one-bedroom apartment in a well-kept building on the twelfth floor. There were large windows on the west side of the building that framed many great sunsets. No matter what time of day, what season it was or what the weather was like you could always enjoy a beautiful and unobstructed picture that was always changing. Even though it was small, it was one of my favorite places to live. And Gina, I felt, was an extremely supportive wife or girlfriend anyone could possibly have. Yeah, I was feeling pretty good about my life.

All along I had been developing my drumming skills and, also the flute. At one point, I think it was Lorenzo who introduced me to musicians who were the sons of an owner of a chain of Spanish-speaking theater. We formed a band to play during the intermissions between the movies. Lorenzo and I were on the percussions and the two brothers Tom and Jerry played guitar and bass. I don't remember when, but at some point, we brough in a trumpet player. The band played mostly Latin music and we later evolved into a band called "The Latin Soul Disciples" (or the LSD band), even though the personnel were mostly Jewish and African American with no Latinos. Eventually we started playing other stuff that might be considered Pop Rock. Later we changed the name to The Messiahs of Handel or "The Moh" for short.

Lorenzo and I had become best buddies, going to pool halls, playing our conga drums, etc. One day he decided he was going to join the Marines. At that time there was still a draft in place, and everyone had to register when they were eighteen. I, of course, was 4F, which meant you weren't physically fit to go into service. Before Lorenzo had a student status but now, he had chosen to enlist. He wasn't really a tough guy, so I was a little surprised he decided on the Marines. I don't remember him going to boot camp, and it seemed in no time he was in Viet Nam. One day when I was at his mother's house, making a recording to send to Lorenzo, a Nigerian gentleman stopped by for a visit. He said his name was Sam Akpobot from Nigeria. In talking to him, he told me he was a musician, and he had a band and would like to invite me to play with them. Honestly, I didn't think much about it, but I did go to their next rehearsal.

As it would turn out Sam had had a successful career in London before I met him. He played the organ and xylophone, and the type of music we played was called African Highlife. I would find out later in my life that Sam was renowned worldwide and an accomplished composer, musician, and author. I feel privileged to have worked with him for the time that I did. We played regularly about two nights a week. We played at clubs and college campuses around the Chicago area and two or three times on Wisconsin or Michigan campuses. After we had played together for a while, we went to an ASCAP (American Society of Composers, Authors, and Publishers) studio. ASCAP offered Sam a five-year contract. As his supporting musicians we were offered a minimum pay of $200 per week and travel expenses paid by ASCAP. Now for a young guy that never made shit, that was a pretty good deal in the 1960's. However, Sam was not planning on staying in the States another five years, so the contract was nixed. Of course, I did realize that might have been a stress on my marriage. C'est la vie.

The band did continue to perform while Sam stayed around, but the thing I enjoyed the most was playing with a Ghanaian drummer called Ben Ali. He was about my height, but muscular and maybe a little cocky. The first time he was invited to a rehearsal, he set up his drums and we began playing. Sam signaled me to solo and as I was soloing Ben gave out a big howl of approval. I know he was sincere because he felt exactly what I was expressing. From that moment on we were best buddies. We loved each other's playing. One time when we were on a gig, the program had completely trashed my name. Instead of "Bobby Hannum" they had spelled something like Bobi Aannam.

On the bus after the gig Ben said to me that "Bobi" was a Ghanaian name, meaning "brother," Aanna meant something else that I can't remember. He suggested that I should change my name to Bobi Aanna. I said, "But my skin is too light, and no one will ever buy it." Although he might have been blowing smoke up my ass, he said in northern Africa there plenty of light –skinned Ghanaians, so I bought it and from that point on that was my name in the band. One time a Gary Indiana, newspaper interviewed me about how I felt playing over here in America being from Ghana. I didn't usually fake an accent but this time I did. The next day they printed my comment in the paper. We would have the best time playing together and most of the time we were high. I really felt like he was my Ghanaian brother.

One of the places we played was a place called the Persian Lounge" which had some big names perform there in its heyday, people like Duke Ellington. It was a very cool place. The stage was on the same level as the bar. In the middle of the stage was a ramp that came forward connecting the stage and the bar. So, a dancer on the stage could dance right onto the bar. On either side of the ramp was a bartender serving the customers.

One night when I was taking a break, a man approached me, who I knew right away. It was Jimmy, from my hometown. Jimmy was maybe two years older than me, but we went to the same schools. As I said before, I grew up in what I thought was a tough guy's world even though I wasn't that tough myself. In my mind Jimmy was one of those guys that I looked up to as being tough. He was stocky in size and looked like he was certainly no pushover. However, he was genuinely a nice guy. It was good to be reconnected with someone from my hometown community. Jimmy also connected me up with a few of my classmates who had also moved to Chicago. Jimmy always seemed to know where all the underground places were. Some of them were rough places. Once we were in one of those joints when things started getting intense. At that point Jimmy instructed me to get back-to-back with him in case we had to fight our way out of there. Well, I knew he had my back, because he had been in one of those military elite groups like the Special Forces, but I wasn't sure that I had his back. However, I had no choice but to give it my best. My best move was to quickly get under a person and lift them while I pulled their legs from under them. I could just hope that I would be successful right away. As it turned out the situation defused. In my heart I had a big sigh of relief. I would have hated to let Jimmy down.

I remember another time when the police came into another joint and started searching everyone. When they searched me, they found a small handgun on me and asked me how much money I had on me. I only had a few dollars and they asked how soon I could get $50 as payment to get my gun back. I told him about two weeks. He said, "two weeks!" Then he walked away. Of course, this was obviously a shakedown. After a while the cops decided to leave. The one that had my gun came over to me, handed the gun to me, and said, "You look like you probably need this," and left. Jimmy would remain my friend for the rest of the time I lived in Chicago. After I left Chicago, I reached out to him once but was never able to contact him again. Years later I tried to find him, but he had moved back to Knoxville and gotten sick, strangely and passed away.

While working at Liberty Photo Engraving, about the only significant experience I had was meeting Chester. Chester was an older Black man who was also a tremendous artist and, among other things, built miniature train cars. At one point he was in an annual publication called Who's Who in America for some of his accomplishments. For sure he was the most talented in the company at that time but in the end, he was holding a low-income job and was another example of the difficulty of overcoming the shackles of being Black in America at the time.

I wasn't content with working at Liberty, so I set out looking for a better job and preferably closer to home. Looking for a job was another opportunity for racism to raise its ugly head. While I was looking for another job, the idea of working in the neighborhood became increasingly appealing to me. Hyde Park was my favorite place in Chicago and the University of Chicago was the largest corporation in Hyde Park. There were plenty of jobs available there. Since Gina was a museum secretary on the campus, she began putting the word out that her husband was looking for work. There were cases where, when Gina would say her husband was looking for work, people would say send him in, and when I would show up there was suddenly nothing available. I was light skinned but with my afro it was obvious I was Black.

One such case was when I showed up at the personnel office after Gina had gotten a green light from one of the employees in that office. They gave me the interview and told me that there was nothing open at that time. Betty who was the sister of two the brothers that I played with and had also dated Lorenzo, my best friend at the time, worked with the woman in charge of the personnel office. Betty described my situation to her, and she told Betty to ask me to come in to talk to her. When I went to see her, I found out that the application for the last interview had described me as "slovenly and belligerent". I guess that was not her opinion because she decided to give me a temporary job as a desk clerk in a dormitory. I liked that job a lot and enjoyed all the students and, with the students it seemed the feeling was mutual. After the temporary position was finished, the director of personnel decided to recommend me for a full-time position and I was hired as an operating room orderly in the Lying Inn Hospital, which was a hospital for gynecology and obstetrics which would be a major chapter in my life. But first allow me to deviate to fill in what was going on in my music world.

Sam Akpobot was a highly respected musical artist in the African community. While I was still playing with Sam, a Liberian by the name of Alex approached me and said he liked my playing and would like to invite me to come and play with a group called the Dukorans. So, when Sam left to go back (I presume to Africa), I joined the Dukorans. The group was led by Alex, who later became the Liberian Consul General in Chicago. He teamed up with a tall muscular African American dancer named Chico who had joined the Sikh Religion and sometimes went by the name of Singh Masala. Chico was motivated to keep working regularly. The ideal we had was to find a place that we could call our home base every Saturday night. The first place we found was upstairs in a place that was popular at one time call Poor Richard's. We called the upstairs the Zimba Room. It was in an artsy area called Old Town Chicago on Wells Street. The show had a pretty good run and we played three sets every Saturday night. Each week there was a definite pattern. The first set was mostly white people from the suburbs, the second set was a little more diverse and the third set a way-funkier crowd consisting of regulars and people from the nearby low-income community, a mostly Black crowd. There were some public housing high-rises nearby that were so dangerous emergency vehicles would need a police escort to enter the buildings. One time Freddy, one of the drummers from Liberia, went home with a girl who lived in one of those high-rises and was found the next morning badly beat up. He was ok in the end.

The Dukorans

The next place we set up shop after the Zimba room gig ended, was a place on Sedgwick Avenue a little further north of

Old Town. Some of us who performed in the show after it came down remodeled the stage area to look like an African village. The door that went backstage was like entering a grass hut. During the day the place was a hangout for young people. While we were working on the place every day all the people who hung out there got to know us. When the opening night came we had already developed a little groupie section. In this place we also had a decent run, but for less time than the Zimba Room ran. It was at this show I met Samson (not his real name). I think Chico had brought him on as a new dancer. He was mediumly tall and extremely muscular. He was a good dancer and a good addition to the show.

One night after the show as I was exiting the backstage area, an attractive older lady (30 to 35) walked up to me and said, "Well are you going with us"? Then I noticed Samson and another woman standing looking in my direction. Now, the correct answer was, "No I need to get home." But what came out of my mouth with no hesitation was "Sure". I was driving, so we proceeded to the apartment of the woman Samson was with. While we were in transit, Samson made a comment as if to be encouraging me to feel confident despite that was a small guy. I assumed that he was expressing some sort of strange one-upmanship, but I wasn't sure and didn't feel like taking any time to think about it. When we got to the one room apartment, after another one of his comments and very little, small-talk, I and the one woman retreated to the only other place available, the bathroom. After we did our thing and talked a few moments, we knocked on the door and came out. Samson apparently had some issues, but I didn't realize to what extent. I don't remember if I dropped him off somewhere but that was the last time, I remember seeing Samson. I heard later that Samson had thrown himself in front of a train and severed both his legs. I think what I saw of Samson's issues were just the tip of the iceberg.

I was also still performing with the pop rock band, The Messiahs of Handel" It was about that time when we got an opportunity to audition at what I think was Pepper's Lounge, possibly the biggest venue for blues in Chicago at the time. This was without a doubt the most exciting audition I had ever experienced. I think it was a Black-owned facility with somewhat diverse clientele. I was the only Black person in the band at the time and from a distance that wasn't very clear. We had a British singer who was extremely soulful. If you were soulful enough and rocked the crowd you were in, they didn't care if you were green.

In that respect it was much like the Apollo Theater in New York. If I remember correctly, we were just setting up for our audition, when a loud ruckus came from the direction of the entrance. Then suddenly a big brawl was in progress. We unplugged all our equipment and began dragging it toward the entrance right through the thick of things. I remember as we were going out of the door, a very big guy with long arms was throwing big punches at somebody. As it turned out, the police apparently had a score to settle with the bouncers and that was what it was all about. Latter we found out they arrested the owner, which I guess made a statement. Needless to say, we didn't get the job and didn't go back.

Working at Lying In

Lying In Hospital was part of a five-hospital complex owned by the University of Chicago. The main hospital was called Billings Hospital which was a general hospital. There was also a children's hospital and two others that I don't remember anything about. Lying In was a Gynecology and Obstetrics facility. I worked on the 5th floor and that was where the operating rooms were along with a full staff that would sterilize, prepare, and package all linen and equipment necessary for a full day of surgeries for two operating rooms. My job was to pick up the first patient due for surgery in the morning and then take the patient to the recovery room and after that, back to their hospital room.

When I wasn't busy transporting patients, it was my job to load up the autoclave (a tank used for sterilization with pressurized steam). I was given pre-wrapped bales, each wrapped to support a specific type of surgery or baby delivery.

The staff was a group of African American women led by Liz. Liz was more than a person in charge; she was like a mom to us all in that department. As a matter of fact, I think we used to sometimes call her mom sometimes. I remember one time she called me over and gave me a bar of soap and told me to take a shower. Coming from her it wasn't really that bad. I was still smoking a lot of weed and I had to be in my scrubs and pick the first patient up at 7am every weekday. I'm sure I missed some showers. One morning when I was standing to the side of the operating table waiting to take a patient off the table, I suddenly hear a voice say "Bobby, Bobby" and I had just zoned out that quickly. I don't want to give the impression that I was irresponsible, because I was a good worker, but I did have my issues. Getting high too much was one of them.

My supervisor was a little Japanese lady named Elsie. Elsie was totally dedicated to her job and totally dedicated to her supervisor and the administration. I on the other hand had a big concern about how the underdog was treated. I think that is not so unusual being Black in our society. This theme would turn out to be major during my stay at Lying In. I remember once Elsie asked me to mop the floors and I told her that our union wouldn't allow it. She said that her supervisor told her to have me do it. I was so impressed with her loyalty that I said to her "If she told you to kill me would do that?" Once she got so frustrated with me that I could hear her in the closet throwing the I.V. bottles around almost to the point I thought the bottles would start breaking. (Before the I.V. bags, there were I.V. bottles).

All the employees were women, except for two orderlies, the doctors, and some house-keeping personnel. That was fine by me because my family for the first 19 years of my life was almost all women. After I really got used to the place, I liked it a lot. I became a horrible flirt. I felt like a kid in a candy store. However, I did have enough sense not to flirt with the patients. That was taboo around the hospital for good reason. I did work with an orderly who did flirt with and even dated a patient. Needless to say. He didn't last long there. The patients were usually under medication and might make a pass at you. I had one woman grab me by the collar with both hands and try to pull me in her bed.

At that time, I was driving a Volvo that was a popular car with the doctors at the hospital and that didn't hurt my reputation at all. One day when Gina came to visit for whatever reason some of the women saw her and began complimenting me about what a cute wife I had. Information spread quite fast in Lying In and my reputation was soaring. The only thing that was growing faster than my reputation was the size of my head. I was getting very much full of myself.

At this time with both Gina and I working fulltime jobs we were living more comfortably than we had since we had been together. Gina attracted a lot of friends. One of those friends was Ken the Philosophy student. Now there was no doubt in my mind that the only reason we were friends was Ken's desire to get into Gina's pants. Of course, I certainly was judging him completely by the likes of myself. But be that as it may, I will say that hanging out with Ken was a lot of fun and exposed me to the likes of, Plato, Aristotle, Nietzsche, Marcus Aurelius, and others. Hyde Park in general was a fun place to live and hang out with people from many different cultures coming there to attend school at the University of Chicago mainly. And I think the three of us made good use of that environment. I remember one time Ken, who was Italian, was going to travel to Italy, which he considered his home country, since he was Italian. There was an Italian restaurant in Hyde Park called Nicky's Pizzeria "which was very popular, but Ken couldn't wait to get to eat some real Italian pizza. When he returned from his very rewarding trip, he expressed his greatest disappointment was to discover that real Italian pizza was nothing more than a small bread crust with a little cheese on it sold on street corners.

One time Gina informed me that Ken along with some of her fellow workers wanted to have a symposium, a Greek idea where people would come together to drink, enjoy music, and exchange ideas. When I asked what a symposium was, I was told basically it is a drinking party. I thought, "No problem, I can do that. The party was to be held at Ken's apartment and he was inviting a few people from the Oriental Institute where Gina and Ken worked. When the party came around it seemed to be a pretty cool group. There were two Black men there, me and the museum curator. As the "symposium progressed I got so drunk that I was smoking a cigar from the wrong end getting ashes in my mouth. Everyone was asked how he or she spent 75% of their time. When they came around to me, I said "Sex". As one might expect, everyone had blank look for about two seconds and then went on to the next person. I was too drunk to even care. The next morning, I woke up in my own apartment with my head on the pipes under the bathroom sink. As I looked up, I saw the curator with his head hanging over into the bathtub. When I got up and walked into the living room, I saw Gina sitting on the couch looking very sober with her legs crossed and gently swinging the leg on top. I could only imagine what she must have been thinking. However, I never got that drunk again.

There was another time when Gina invited a friend over from her job and during her very pleasant visit, a friend of mine stopped by so drunk and obnoxious we had to ask him to leave. Since he wouldn't leave, I ended up having to physically remove him and doing so I slammed the door on his hand. I felt very bad about that, but I never saw him again.

Well, there was another time when the Oriental Institute gave a masquerade party, and I got quite drunk there, too. I remember I was watching this one guy who had on a Turkish outfit. As I was watching the big red, yellow, and orange feather sticking out of his turban, I really became infatuated with how the light was hitting the feathers. They seemed to be getting more and more brilliant and I was in awe of them. Then suddenly someone abruptly started furiously patting his head and I realized that the intensely beautiful colors I saw were in fact his feathers catching on fire.

I don't mean to imply that me and/or my friends would always trash Gina's social events. After all there was the sweet Egyptian woman who introduced me to yogurt with her yogurt-grape dessert. And there was the cool couple who looked like Bjorn Borg and Natalie Wood who also left his telescope with me when they went away for a few months (and I literally, saw Saturn one night when I was playing with it). However, the above events are the ones I remember most.

A lot of things happened while I was at Lying In, and some were even life changing. It was there that I had what I thought was the worst day of my life. It's not that something had devastated me for the rest of my life, but it was just a bad day from beginning to the end. It was a Christmas Eve and right off the bat I took a sleeping capsule to get a little buzz, I that I think was called Seconal. When I got to my department the ladies had a Christmas cake, preparing for the Christmas party. I walked in without noticing the cake leaned over and stuck my elbow right in the cake. As the day went on, I accidently knocked the remaining half of the cake onto the floor. That night I had a gig at a Christmas party in a hotel. I needed to get there early so we could set up the equipment. As I was unloading an amplifier from my car in the underground parking lot of the hotel, I dropped it on my foot. If I remember correctly, when I was bringing my equipment up the elevator there was an obnoxious guy on the elevator talking loud and had obviously been drinking. In any event I went in the ballroom, and we set up the band.

After that I went to the bar. You would think after the day

I had because of the Seconal; the bar would have been the last place I would go. But that was not the case. After we played our first set, I noticed that my obnoxious friend from the elevator had found his way to the party. You would think staying away from that guy would have been a priority, but no, I walked right over to the bar where he was. Of course, my judgment wasn't that great after the Seconal and the drinking. In any case we got into a conversation that soon became an argument and then an all-out physical altercation. Now from my perspective, all I remember was getting so livid that I just jumped onto his chest. Then, in what seemed like a split second, I heard shattering glass and then about two maybe three guys were holding me over their heads. That's literally all I remember. When they let me down, I remember seeing the kitchen help standing there who had all come out of the kitchen investigating the ruckus.

I noticed they were all Black, which in a way was kind of comforting since I didn't see any other Black folk there, and even though I don't remember what we were arguing about, I think it was racial. Because I was so drunk, I wouldn't trust my judgment. The security escorted the obnoxious guy to the door and when the dust cleared someone asked, "Are you ok?" When I looked up it was a girl who was, I think, a modern dancer who I had hung out with a few times and picked up at her dance studio maybe a couple of times. And, I might add, someone I shouldn't have been hanging out with at all. I then said, "Sure, I'm ok". She then asked me did that kind of thing happen to me often. I don't remember my response but of course that was literally a once in a lifetime experience. After the gig when I was on my way home, I was so intoxicated I had to pull over and rest a bit before I could proceed.

When I was exiting the parking space, I ran into the bumper of a car parked in front of me. When I got back on the road, I was then stopped by a traffic cop because of my erratic driving. After I told him how close I was from my home he decided to let me go because he knew I would be in big trouble if he took me in. When I got home that was the happiest moment of that day. The next day one of the band members came over to check up on me and he said that the other guy had slammed his glass to the floor as if to say let me take care of this little guy but could never get me down. I wasn't sure how to take that, I was just glad I got through that day alive. Oh yeah, I never took that drug again.

One day when I came to work a young man was coming down the hall saying, "We're going to strike.". I think his name was Raymond. Raymond had been there a while and knew the political atmosphere surrounding the hospitals on campus. After talking to Raymond, I was impressed with the low pay of many of the employees, particularly the housekeeping department.

The University of Chicago was considered one of the richest institutions in Chicago and I felt it was very unfair for an organization that size to pay such low wages. Because of that situation, there was some unrest around the complex of hospitals, and I became very sympathetic with the workers. To address the issue the administration decided to call a meeting with the employees. Just prior to the meeting, some of the supervisors met with the housekeeping personnel over refreshments and discouraged them from attending the meeting with the administration. When the meeting started, I didn't see any of the housekeeping staff at the meeting. I immediately started running around the hospital to gather them up. That's when I found out they had been told not to come. They were all afraid to come. I felt that was a very cruel thing to do to the people who were at the very center of the issue. Because of the time I took to try and gather up the people from housekeeping, I was late for the meeting. I was extremely angry at what I thought was an underhanded way to defuse the situation. When I got to the auditorium, I burst through the double doors loudly expressing my disdain for the administration's dishonest pretense of having that meeting. I don't remember exactly what I said but I do remember telling them they were very underhanded in their approach, and they could fire me and then I walked out the door saying, "We're only human." I was told that after I walked out, a few people asked some pointed questions to the administration and not being satisfied with their answers, began walking out. Eventually people started filing out at such a rate that the meeting ended.

Now the question was how do we respond to the current situation?" I then remembered the girl who asked me to teach her to play the flute and I remembered that she was also a member of SDS (Students for a Democratic Society). The SDS had some experience organizing strikes. I went to her and promised her flute lessons if she would help me out. To my amazement, the next morning when I got to work the students were handing out signs to the workers and we had an all-out strike going on.
This all was the beginning of a whole new social awareness for me. I was surprised at myself for taking responsibility for making sure that the employees in the housekeeping department were at that meeting. With no hesitation I was motivated passionately to fight an injustice. Wow!

If I remember correctly, the strike lasted two, maybe three days. We were out there with picket signs, stopping trucks from delivering supplies. However, in retrospect that probably wasn't the brightest thing we did. After all I had no experience in this area and had not thought things through. Another problem was that there was no clear leader on the side of the workers. When the news media came out, they of course got all their information from the administration representing the hospitals. I looked to Raymond as the person who got me started. But during the strike I never saw him and didn't know how to get in touch with him. It all happened so fast we really didn't have time to organize.

I think we got some small concessions by the hospital administration to bring the strike to a halt. However, there was a lot more to get done. It was necessary to get organized. Therefore, we started turning to the union. I and a few other workers began attending the union meetings. As it turned out many of the older employees looked at us as troublemakers. There was a clear division among the union members. I'm not sure if it was time to re-elect the union president or whether the idea came up to resolve the issue but that is exactly what it came down to. Raymond on our side was running against a guy named Charles (I think) who was the incumbent. It was a hard-fought election but, in the end, we lost the election. Of course, the administration did everything they could to protect their interest. So, that being said, the issue was resolved.

The "Party"

After the strike and the election were over, I still was hanging out with the SDS organization. My hunger to fight for social justice had certainly been awakened. The SDS was going through a transition. They split up into two factions. The most militant was called the Weathermen and I don't remember what the other one was called. In any case, through the Weathermen, I was introduced to some members of the Black Panther Party. The Party was started by Huey Newton and Bobby Seale in Oakland, CA. It grew out of the injustices experienced in the Black communities and its goal was to organize the masses to establish a socialist revolution. It advocated arming oneself and depending only on yourself to protect yourself during this revolutionary transition. The Party solicited the community for those who could donate time and supplies to help develop community-based programs such as free breakfasts and health care for those who couldn't afford it. They networked with other groups of similar interest such as SDS, "The Young Lords, The White Panthers, and others. However, at that time in the news media the Party was depicted as a racist street gang. Once I attended my first Black Panther Party meeting, I was hooked.

During this period of social awakening, some serious things were also taking place in my personal life. As I mentioned before, I was a terrible flirt. I was constantly making passes at women, but very rarely did anything go beyond that. One such case that did go beyond the flirting stage was that of Bee. Bee was a good-looking dark-skinned woman who seemed to enjoy thinking of herself as a "tough sister". She would brag about her brothers teaching her to be tough. During the strike and attending union meetings we were together a lot. So, as it turned out, our relationship developed into an all-out affair. Bee had a slightly possessive personality and would always remind me that she was my Number Two woman and I better not let her catch me with a Number Three.

Meanwhile, the band I was playing with, the Messiahs of Handel or MOH for short, was being managed by Bobbie, who was a 31-year-old woman that I always thought of as an older woman because I was 24, maybe 25. Anyway, she was the woman in charge, and I felt it was my duty to make a subtle pass at her every opportunity I had. I remember thinking at one point "What do I need to say to her to close the deal?" At my first opportunity I said to her what I thought would make the difference and "Voilà." I don't remember what I said to her, but she said later that it was exactly what she needed to hear from me to move forward. I remember us getting into the back seat of the car on the way to the gigs, putting a coat over us and having private fun under the coat. Of course, I was having a pretty good time massaging my ego but inevitably it was all to come to an end.

The Moh

One day, if I remember correctly, I had gotten my schedule screwed up. I was with Bee and had planned to see Bobbie that evening. However, I needed to get home to avoid being out too late. I remember parking my car and rushing down the street toward Bobbie's place, being out of breath and frantic, when I suddenly realized that I was totally out of control and in way over my head. Meanwhile, on my job Bee, who had overheard me talking to Bobbie on the phone, was giving me a lot of shit about it. This fantasy seemed to be turning into a bad dream. But little did I know that the worst was yet to come.

One other day when I was at work, I was just entering our main work area on the 5th floor and all the women were standing around. When I walked through the doorway, suddenly Bee came out of nowhere and started attacking me. I assumed that she was kidding around but she was very relentless. Now Bee was the type of person that you couldn't tell by just looking at her face, which always seemed sort of serious. I remember saying, "Baby what are you doing?" I was saying stuff like, "Bee, calm down". I finally managed to get behind her and lock my arms around her and lifted her off her feet while pinning her arms to her side. In a few seconds she calmed down. I then released her, and she abruptly walked away. I was standing there catching my breath when I heard one of the women say "Aw, she didn't get him". And then another woman said," No, but it took everything he had to keep her off him." From those two statements I concluded that she had the women standing around to watch as she humiliated me. At that point it was clear to me that a relationship with Dee was way too much work for me. I don't think we ever got together again.

On what I think was a weekend, the band was supposed to get together for some reason, however, I had arranged to see Bobbie at her place. She didn't live very far away from us and I'm sure I told Gina I would be with the band members. I have no idea how long I was there but I'm sure it was a longer time than it appeared to me. In any case, I had to get home and she had to leave. When we left her place, I walked her to her car. She got into the car on the driver's side, and I was saying my goodbyes from the passenger's side. I remember saying, "See you later, Killer" (killer a term of endearment from the term "lady killer" or in her case "man killer"). As I straightened up noticing a figure to my left, I looked up to see Gina. Now, what I am going to describe, happened in about one second but seemed like an eternity. When I saw her, I had two distinct thoughts, they were "Damn she looks good" and "Shit I'm going to lose her". Her hair was pulled back into two braids sort of a Native American style, and she wore some colorful tight pants. Then what came out of her mouth was, "You mother fucker", a term I had never heard her use, at least not seriously. Then the next thing that came from her mouth was, "I'm going to leave your ass", and I knew she meant it.

From that moment until we got home is completely blank in my mind. I do know however that it was one of the most depressing periods of my life and I'm sure very little was said on my part. As it turns out, Bobbie had given me some "acid" (LSD, a popular recreational drug at the time). Taking acid was called tripping because when you took it you were in for a virtual trip. An acid trip might last for some hours getting more and more intense at first, and then gradually bringing you back to reality. Sometimes a person may not make it back from a trip completely. And that was exactly what happened to a friend of mine. He was a young freshman in college majoring in philosophy with an extremely promising future. He took his first hit of acid and never completely returned mentally. His promising future was over. Gina was getting high by this time but that was not always the case. I think it was about a year into our marriage when she busted me with some grass and was very upset, declaring that I was doomed to die. I don't know if she had talked to someone or did some research, but shortly after that she came to me and said with a very stern look, let me try that stuff (as if to say, "Let me see what you're getting yourself into"). But of course, once she tried it, she became my favorite smoking buddy.

As I said before, I remember no conversation we might have had after we left Bobbie's place but somehow, we decided to take the acid. With all the cards stacked against me that was probably the best decision I made that day. Now with acid there are good trips and bad ones. (At this point let me go on record as saying that I would not advise anyone to experiment with that drug because I know of no way to determine, beforehand what kind of trip it might be, and the bad trips could be horrifying.) I think it was both the combination of the effects of the drug and the emotional rollercoaster we were both going through. Gina was more passionate than I ever remember her, and I was so glad that she was still around, and I really appreciated the moment. I certainly had tripped before on numerous occasions, but nothing could even compare with that. That was an evening to remember. I think that trip extended our marriage. And the affaires with Bobbie and Bee were over. I think it was the next morning when we had landed that Gina asked me to promise that we would never take acid with anyone else, and I did just that.

The day after our trip was also a day to remember. I was repairing the electric cord on an iron when I accidentally sliced my finger with a razorblade. It was the middle finger on my left hand, and it was bleeding severely. All we could do was to wrap my hand as best we could and rush to the hospital's emergency room. When we got to the emergency room and were checking in, we looked up and discovered that Bobbie was also there. Apparently, she had overdosed (on probably the same stuff that she gave to me) and had to check in for help. What happened next just got more bizarre. Gina began talking loudly and trying to get to Bobbie. Remember my hand was wrapped in a bloody towel and I was trying to hold Gina. Finally, she convinced me that she wasn't going to do anything, and I let her go, hoping to defuse the situation. She went across this large room and said something in her face and came back. She then said, "I just thanked her for the trip". I never seriously thought about the sayings, "What goes around comes around", "You reap what you sow," etc. but the events of those two days showed a good example of proof supporting that concept.

A few days later I called Bobbie to tell her that I would no longer be seeing her and that would also mean I would no longer be in the band. When she first answered, she said "If you wanted to keep seeing me you should've called me sooner". I then informed her why I had really called and then she made a comment that Gina looked nothing like she had perceived her to look. I wasn't sure how to take that, but Gina was looking pretty good when she busted us, so I just left it at that. I don't remember seeing Bobbie again. At the time I was busted, Bobbie and I were supposed to be at a gathering with the band. So, I always assumed that some of the band members told Gina where I was. As it turns out I was wrong. She had just gone for a walk in the neighborhood and spotted our car.

As I had said before, the lustful evening with the acid trip did help us to move forward but I had hurt her bad and there were some seriously unresolved issues. Gina had never been anything other than a supportive wife to me and was never boring to me in any way. I didn't have the slightest excuse for my actions that led us to this place. From my perspective, she was just trying to cope with the world that I had created for us, and I desperately wanted to hang on to her. So, I don't remember the conversations we had, but our conclusion was, turnabout is fair play and there was a high likelihood that it was my suggestion. I was feeling confident in myself and thinking I would have no problem handling anything, so, the first thing she did was to hook up with Rick the drummer and the youngest member in the band. Of course, the reality of it was not quite as easy as I thought.

It is very true that there was a lot going on, on the home front, however there was a lot going on outside of the home also. By this time, I was spending a lot of time with the Black Panther Party. It all began when I first attended a rally. That's where I first saw "The Chairman". Fred Hampton was the Chairman of the Chicago branch of the BPP. He was 21 years old at that time and was the most dynamic young man that I had personally met. The rally was held in a church or maybe a community center and maybe 100-200 people were there. Then three young men came to the stage, the first and the third carried shotguns. As the Chairman who was in the middle came to the center of the stage the other two men faced outward to protect the Chairman. One of the young men was Bobby Rush who later became a congressman. I don't remember who the other one was. When the Chairman spoke, he was so clear so powerful and delivered his message in a down to earth street language. He stressed the Second Amendment (the right to bear arms) and taught the empowerment of the masses. I was so pumped when I came out of there, I was ready to take on the corporate world by myself.

There was some very strict training to become a Black Panther, a criterion that I never really met. I believed however wholehearted in what they were doing, and I certainly wanted to help. I wasn't the only one who wanted to support, more and more people started to lend their support also. I remember once when my tooth started bothering me, they sent me to a dentist. He asked me was I supporting the movement when he fixed my tooth. I told him absolutely, so he didn't charge me. They had one or two apartments outside of the main office that they carried on activities from, and one of which I would do watch duty from time to time. I recall being on watch in this apartment with this mattress covering the window with tin foil covering the mattress on the outside. I remember thinking if the police started shooting through that thing, I would be chopped liver. Being in one of those places was a real danger because the Chicago Police Chief would send his policemen to shoot up these facilities. The problem was that nobody really believed that it was happening (except for the people that lived in those communities).

Another way I could help was transportation. There only seemed to be a limited number of cars availably to the movement. Since I was one of the few cars available to the Party, I would be tailed a lot by the FBI. They would not even try to be inconspicuous. They would drive next to us taking pictures and making comments. One time I had a couple of joints in my pocket. Trying to lose them I would go slow until the traffic light would turn yellow, then I would accelerate, and they would just come through the red light. I then threw the two joints in my mouth and ate them. Then they drove up beside me and said, "you might as well tell us where you're going, you're not getting away" and I said, "I'm just going for a ride, you're welcome to come". They then laughed and drove off. They would offer to help us carry boxes when we would carry them from the office. Sometimes we would sing "Piggy Wiggy you got to go" as they took our picture. I never feared the FBI, in some ways I sort of related to them. It was as if we, and them were in this underground game that most people didn't know about. On the other hand, the Chicago police was someone to fear.

Philosophically the Party was a socialistic movement. Much of their ideology came directly from the "Red Book" of Mao Zedong (Chairman Mao), which they studied diligently. I even recall hearing some white women from the suburbs considering socialism in a positive light. Of course, the greatest support came from the Black, Hispanic and poor communities. It is true however that the media had conducted a reasonably successful campaign to paint the Party as a racist organization. During the time I participated in the Party's activities, I never saw the slightest evidence of racism on the Panther's part.

One time there was a young black man who was wanted by the local authorities. He was beginning to become somewhat of a hero in the community. The Party wanted to protect him, and we kept him at our place for maybe one or two nights. That was an intense movement. When I came home in the evening I had to knock on the door, the door would open with all the lights out inside and several shotguns pointed at me until I was identified. Now if the situation wasn't bad enough, one of those nights Rick the young drummer showed up drunk and started getting a little loud. Then "Ben", a big dark complexioned, quiet guy with thick glasses, said he could knock the kid out in a couple of seconds, to quieten him down. As I thought about that, the picture of four black dudes, one a fugitive, with a white woman and a young dead blonde, white kid, was not sitting too well with me. I figured Gina could handle the situation much more efficiently. She left with him, came back in a short time and the situation was handled. After it was all over, I found out that one of our neighbors had interrupted Gina and Rick while they were handling the situation in the stairwell. All in all, that was one of the most intense evenings of my life. In a few days the young fugitive and his protectors had moved on.

One of the activities available was the breakfast program. That was a program to feed people such as the homeless and people that may be having trouble feeding their kids etc. During the day I was working at the hospital. Another activity that I would have loved to be a part of was the medical program. The medical programs were headed up by a young mild-mannered man, who was hardly any bigger than I was. They called him "Doc". Gina described him as a "real charmer". He was very polite, communicated well and I think aspired to becoming a doctor. I hope he was able to fulfill that dream.

The Party was really becoming a major part of my life. I had become a part of the dream. I had been to the Chairman's house once, maybe twice and it was obvious that he was living as he preached. He lived in a very moderate house (Actually I think it was an apartment but, in my mind, I always remember it as a house) shared by a few people that were close to him and, also a part of the movement. On December 3, 1969, we had a rally.

He was at the top of his game as he usually was at these rallies. Sometimes after these events he would call on some of the men to stick around after the event. I was never one of them. One day I was allowed to stick around but as a witness only participant. It became clear why I was never asked to participate. He put the young men through some very rigorous physical and mental training. He was calling out commands striking them on the back with 2x4 pieces of wood etc. I was of course too small and fragile to handle that. He seemed to be very aware of what they could take, and to my knowledge nobody got hurt. I was 25 years old, and he was 21, but that young man was my hero.

One morning (Thursday the 25th) while I was at work, I heard on the news that Fred Hampton had been killed. The word was, that there had been a shootout with the Chicago police, and he was one of the ones who died. As you could imagine I was upset, I was still pumped from his motivation the night before. I was so upset that I asked to leave work early. As I was leaving my job and walking to the car, an obvious FBI agent was taking pictures of me as he stood outside a big black Lincoln Continental. This was a pretty dark day.

What happened after that was nothing short of extraordinary. Of course, the story being told by the media was about this shootout between the Panthers and the police with the Panthers opening fire to avoid being searched for the possession of weapons. The people in the house said that they were all sleep when a barrage of bullet fire began penetrating the walls and there was only one shot came from the inside. Edward Harahan, the Chicago Police chief, held a news conference showing photos to support his claims. In the photos he had circled what he claimed to be the bullet holes from the shots that came from the inside of the apartment. However, the Party opened the home to the public. With lines of people around the block they showed the public that what was called bullet holes from the inside were not bullet holes at all, but rather nail heads. In the end all valid investigations lead to a planned assassination probably a collaboration of the FBI and local police. It was in fact 1st degree murder that no one ever served time for. A few good things did happen because of his death, Edward Harahan's lost his job and his political career, and some party members began to fight with our current broken system etc. but for the most part that movement of the people was halted.

Fred's main goal was the empowerment of the masses, as was constantly expressed in the declaration of "Power to the People". Today there is the biggest economic gap between the masses of people and those in control than ever before. Until the people realize the power is in their hands and unify there will be no change.

Black is beautiful, good hair/bad hair etc.

During this period of the 60s there was another, and maybe more important revolution going on in the Black community. If you recall when I first returned to school after being homebound from my illness, the young girls who I would pass by, would make passes at me when I was walking to school and I said it was because I had light skin. Well, this was all during the 50s when television was new in black and white, the media consisted mainly of newspaper, magazines, movies, billboards, and radio. All of this was almost entirely controlled by white Americans. Everything good was white and black represented everything that what's negative (it seemed). The only time you would see black people in the movies were in buffoon-type roles. I guess you could say that by the time I came on the scene many Black people had developed a strong slave-type mentality with very few exceptions. If your hair was straight, it was good hair; if it was kinky, it was bad hair, and that's exactly the way they referred to it. "Oh, she's got good hair" which meant her hair was straighter than most African American hair. That kind of thinking was entrenched in the Black community but by the 60s and the civil rights movement Black people were standing up and doing something about it. To break the Black community from those chains, Black leaders started coming up with slogans like, "Black is beautiful" or as Jesse Jackson made famous, "I am somebody." at that time wearing an Afro or wearing your hair "natural" was a big deal, in a good way. They literally turned the image around and had beautiful Black women with big fluffy afros. When I was a kid, it was just accepted that all Black women in my community would straighten their hair if it was not already straight. Today the self-image of the African American community may not be perfect, but it has certainly come a long way from where it was when I was a kid. And besides, overcoming adversity just makes you stronger. And the members of the Black American community have certainly overcome a lot of adversity and still have many challenges that could be improved upon.

Leaving the High-Rise

I never went back to the Art Institute. Over the years, music had taken on a big part of my life. Desperately needing a change in my life, I applied for a loan to attend music school. To my amazement, when I received a reply from my request for the loan, it was an approval for a grant. I think that at that time there was a push to make a college education more available to the Black community and I was able to take advantage of it. Whatever the case, I started attending music school at Chicago Music College, which was a part of Roosevelt University. Although I'm not clear about the details of this transition, I was going to attend school full-time, and I would have to get a part-time job to be able to do that.

Chicago Music College did not have quite the romance and glamour of the Art Institute, but it was a solid music school and one of the top music schools in Chicago. But in my mind, the greatest thing that happen to me at the CMC was meeting David Grilly. My first impression of David was a person who took on big musical challenges with a humorous attitude, and maybe slightly nutty. I first remember him in my piano class when he was giving a demonstration on the piano that was more advanced than anything anyone else was doing, but not doing it very well. His attempt was humorous and brought the class to laughter. But David didn't seem to mind. One day David handed me a card. On the card was written the phrase "Nam-myoho-renge-kyo". He showed me how to say the words and said that by saying those words I could have anything I wanted. So, I said something like "Okay I'll check it out" and stuck the card in my pocket. When I was on my way home on the Illinois Central commuter train, I thought about the card. Like I said, David appeared a little nuts to me. But I did remember how he seemed to really believe what he was telling me. So, I pulled the card out of my pocket and read the words under my breath. When I looked up, I met the eyes of a gorgeous dark-haired woman across the aisle facing me who flashed me a great smile. My first thought was, "Damn, what the fuck is this shit". But after that, thinking it was all a little silly and I was being gullible, I didn't think of it anymore.

At this stage of my life, with all I had gone through with my marriage, one would think that chasing other women would be the last thing on my mind. But that was not the case.

One day I had run into an old friend from the Art Institute (whose name was Fee, my old buddy from the Art Institute) who was attending another more commercially oriented art school. He was showing me his school catalog when I ran across a picture of a nude model in a drawing class. This model was nothing like the models at the Art Institute. She was gorgeous. She looked like a model in one of those perfume commercials. Now the next thing I did was nothing short of incorrigible and a first, even for me. I forgot her name, so I will call her Dot. I got the location of the school from my friend and went there during regular hours and told someone in authority that I wanted to see her after her class break. When she came out of the class, she came toward me looking bewildered. I told her that I had seen a picture of her and that I had to meet her. She then said, "What is it that made you feel that you had to meet me?" I then gave her a look as if to say, "Are you serious?" But instead, I said, "Dot, it was a picture." Then she laughed, and we proceeded to have lunch in the cafeteria. I don't remember whether I got her number, but there is no way I would have forgotten that. But whatever the case, I ran into her in the lounge of Roosevelt University where she was apparently taking some courses. When we saw each other, we hung out and talked for what was probably a couple of hours. It was starting to get late, so after some fun conversation I asked could I go home with her. She paused then looked into my eyes as if to read me. This was clearly a test and as I was looking into her eyes, I started thinking about what kind of lie I was going to have to tell Gina and how long this was going to take. Also, of course my guilt was running rampant. And then I choked and looked down. She then said, "No I don't think so" and that was that. In a way I was relieved and thought I was probably about to get in way over my head. I never saw her again. I'm sure it was for the best.

Going to CMC was a rewarding experience. I was studying and learning music. I went to classes during the day and then to my part-time job as a counselor for preschoolers at a day care center until late afternoon. I would mostly entertain them with my flute. To signal when it was time to clean up for the end of the day, I would just start playing "The Party's Over." They would always respond with a big sigh of disappointment. I really liked those kids, and I had a lot of fun with them. They wore their hearts on their chest and what they felt was what you got.

There was one experience during that period that should not be omitted. One day when I was pulling up to the day care center, I saw Gina in front of the center swinging her purse at a young black kid, about 12 or 13 years of age, while he was in a boxing stance taunting her. When I saw them, I instantly felt that I understood how he perceived her as a white woman, not much bigger than he was and representing the enemy. However, I saw him as humiliating my wife. I then jumped out of the car, grabbing a short cane I always carried next to me. When I jumped out of the car, I yelled "Hey," as I was running toward him. He ran away quickly and after a few yards it was clear that I was not going to catch that kid. I felt right away that he had probably slapped her butt, but as she said later, "If I had a nickel for every time a young Black kid had tagged my ass on the subway, I'd be rich." To think of it now is kind of funny, but then the most disturbing thing was my reaction. Inside that cane was a short sword. What was I going to do? Granted it happened very quickly but I had to instantly know what I grabbed. I have thought many times about that incident, often comparing my reaction to the overreaction of a white cop. I would not have recognized that kid but for a short time after that event when I stepped into a neighborhood store or restaurant this kid would suddenly break and run. After a few times I realized it was the same kid. I'm so appreciative that it did not mushroom into anything significant. Really, I could see myself doing something similar when I was a kid, showing off in front of other kids.

I wasn't making much money at the time including my gigs. One day I was so broke, and I only had some change in my pocket, and I needed to call Gina. I don't remember why it was so important for me to call Gina, but I just remember the sense of urgency. I put the change in a pay phone to call Gina, but the phone took my money. It was near the end of the day, and everyone had gone home. I ran back into the interior of the building looking for someone to borrow enough money to call Gina, but no one was there. Then I ran back toward the lounge before everyone had gone home. On the way back to the lounge, I saw what looked like a twenty-dollar bill. I figured it was probably one of those ads that look like a twenty-dollar but when you pick it up you would see an ad on the back. But it was a real twenty-dollar bill.

What are the odds that I would find that money at a time when I so desperately needed it? However, thinking of it as a coincidence I forgot about it.

I only went to CMC for one year, and by the end of the school year I was smoking grass quite regularly. To me, the biggest problem with smoking grass was its quality of being such a de-motivator. It's hard to know how much my getting high influenced motivation for continuing school. At one time I said I'd rather be a starving musician than be anything else. But, remembering some of those nights in Woodlawn when I had nothing, made being a starving anything not an option.

I'm not sure of the exact details of our leaving the high-rise but we certainly needed to cut our expenses and I was going to be in school full-time. Gina had decided with two other young women to share an apartment with us. To me the building looked like a sort of hippie, semi- communal style of living, and it was inexpensive. There were three floors and two apartments on each floor. We were on the first floor. In our apartment there were three bedrooms and a larger family room. I think there was a front and a back entrance, but I never remember using the front one. Gina and I rented the apartment with the two roommates, Betty, and Kathy, who shared the rent. Betty was the sister of the two guitarists in the band (Tom and Jerry) and Kathy was a friend of Gina's from her job (I think).

The apartment was, of course, painted when we moved in, so we decided to have a little fun with our bedroom. We painted all the walls and the ceiling flat black. We painted the wooden floor, the window frames, the windowsill, the frames around the two doors and the doorknobs with bright red enamel. In the middle of the room hung an electric light bulb, which we covered with a big red Chinese lantern. There was a chest of drawers in the room also painted flat black with red outlines around the drawers and on the top surface of the chest. We put vertical mirrors around the walls. When one would turn on the light shining through the red lantern at night everything would disappear except for the floors, window frames and the outline of the doors and draws. It was a great room to get high and/or whatever. I had also planned to paint the ceiling of the family room flat black with invisible stars that could only be seen with black light. But that didn't materialize.

This new place was certainly a change. Where the high-rise tenants were like faculty and staff members from the University of Chicago and in this place were younger people with a much more informal lifestyle. I remember kids playing baseball in the back and one girl stood out. She was about 12 years old somewhat of a tomboy. She lived with an older woman that I wasn't sure if it was her mother or grandmother, but she was a very good ballplayer. Each apartment, on all three floors had its own back porch with handrails around it. Sometimes we were all on our porches watching the kids playing ball. It was sort of a communal atmosphere.

By moving into that apartment our lifestyles did change somewhat. I was still getting high a lot and was taking more hallucinogenic drugs, mostly mescaline (probably of the synthetic type). We decided to buy some bikes. The first time I brought a bike home I chained it to a pole and about ten minutes later I came back to see the bike gone and the chain cut and lying on the ground. I did two things in response to that. I got a heavy-duty bike cable and secondly, I kept my new bike inside. We worked in the neighborhood and Gina rode her bike to work. I rode my bike to work a few times but mostly I drove. I remember when I first got it and was test-driving my bike after I had just taken some mescaline. I was mostly riding in the Co-op parking lot, which came right up to the gate of our back yard. I hadn't been on a bike in a long time, and I felt like a bird flying. I rode around sort of briskly and then slowed way down to almost a complete stop and when the bike would feel like it was falling, I would speed up again, giving the feeling of soaring and diving in the air.

I don't know how long I did that, but it seemed like a long time. That was a good way to become one with my bike. When Betty and Kathy moved in it was a real pleasure and I felt good about the whole change.

Things for the most part seemed to be going smooth, but it wasn't very long before they set me down and talked about my attitude. I guess my initial feeling was that I was being picked on. As I recall it was mostly Betty and Kathy doing the talking. After all Gina had lived with me for years. I do think I took it to heart, but if I had known myself then as I do now, I probably would have been cheering them on. I don't remember the details of what they had to say but I'm pretty sure that my self-centeredness, my disrespect for their opinions and the general chauvinistic attitude that men in our society learn at a very early age had something to do with it.

I'm sure I was expecting a nice fresh change in lifestyle, but I brought all my dirty laundry with me as we all do. I was getting high more than ever. Gina was still seeing her young boyfriend and although I thought I could handle it, it was starting to get to me. One time we were very high, probably from mescaline, and we were lying there having fun. Then in an instant I saw her laughing and somehow, I interpreted the event as her laughing at me. Then, with a burst of anger I slapped her, but almost immediately I saw the surprise in her face making me realize that I had just lost it and I began apologizing profusely. Then her lip started swelling and by this time I was feeling very small and quickly getting more depressed. I was thinking thoughts like, "Our marriage is coming to an end, and I don't have the mental stability to change the direction." At that point I guess we were trying to have an open marriage, but it was wearing on me.

There were a couple of times Gina made arrangement to get together with Rick, her friend. The first time as I recall, I just hung out with Kathy who would never betray Gina but was comforting me in my anguish. During that period my ego was taking a beating. The next time they went out I remembered a phone number of a very cute, young Italian girl who was one of two young girls that my friend Kenny, a Jewish kid, and I had picked up while cruising, (a popular activity with young people in Chicago at the time). I called her and invited her to come and hang out, which she did. I then brought her to our apartment.

My actions had two motivations, one was to make myself feel better and the other was to appear more confident in Kathy's eyes. Both of which was all about my ego and neither made me feel better. After introducing her to Kathy, we proceeded to our bedroom. I estimated the young girl to be about 18 to 20 years of age. However, when we went back into our bedroom and started making out, because of her lack of experience, I believed that she might be even younger than that. In any case after a little petting and joking around, in an effort not to offend her, I told her I had a good time and took her home. Other than a couple of phone calls I don't remember seeing her again. I don't think I ever knew when Gina's fling with Rick ended and I didn't ask, but after a while he just didn't seem to be in the picture.

At one point Betty moved out, I think to go to California, and my friend Kenny moved in her room. He was a good fit at the time and if I'm not mistaken, he was looking to get out of his parent's house. He was young but he had our trust.

The tenants of the building interacted with each other a lot. Sometimes we would all sit on our back porches and watch the kids play ball. After we had been there a while a friend and co-worker of Gina's, Jenise and Phil, her boyfriend, moved into the apartment right next to us. Phil was a musician and the brother of Buddy Guy, the famous blues artist. I was still working on my sax playing but I was not really that good. I did however get a chance to practice with him to improve. Once they had a gig in Toronto, Canada, and invited us to tag along. So, we did go with them, and it was a very fun experience. I noticed that there didn't seem to be as much social tension there, as it was here in the States. When we entered the country, it was way easier to pass inspections at the border than it was coming back. Also, no one seemed to care if you were getting high. Of course, that was 1969 or 1970 and I don't know how it is there now.

Living in a building that had a reputation for having a somewhat communal atmosphere, did have some issues. I'm pretty sure that most everyone in the building probably got high one way or another, and that fact certainly attracted the police when they didn't have anything else to do. I had been arrested a couple of times, once for double parking on Christmas Eve while driving with a suspended license and the other for having a small amount of grass after a random search by the police. I think, in Chicago at the time if you got a traffic ticket your license would automatically be suspended until your court date. Therefore, you could say that it was a bit of an overreaction to arrest me for double parking under those circumstances, and I was released a short time after I got to the police station. With the possession charge, I did have to go to court, but the judge asked the officer why he stopped me, and his answer was that he smelled the marijuana smoke on me. Since the judge did not consider that a legitimate reason to stop and search me the case was dismissed. However, up until then I had never been raided in my house. Well, that would change.

On the west side of our building, which was also the side of our apartment, was an alley where the sanitation trucks would come to pick up the garbage. In hindsight I remember noticing a police car sitting in that alley on more than one occasion. One evening two plain clothes policemen entered the apartment flashing their badges and announcing that we were being raided. They looked around a bit and asked me did we have any drugs. I told them "No, but please feel free to look where they wanted to." They seemed to believe me but halfheartedly walked in our bedroom and looked in the top drawer of our chest of drawers and bingo! There was a bag of grass. The cop that seemed to be in charge looked at me and said, "You know, I believed you," as if he was disappointed in me. At that point I admitted that it was mine. After a quiet conversation with his partner, he asked to speak to Gina alone. What he did was offer to let us go if she would give them sexual favors. After she refused, they arrested her. Before they took her away, I reiterated that the stuff was mine, but they took her anyway. Of course, I had to go get her that night. I don't remember the time that lapsed before we saw a judge but when we did see a judge I was asked, "Did you tell the officer that the drugs belonged to you?" I then said "Yes," and the case was dismissed.

I am pretty sure by this time we were at the very least considering moving out of the building. However, before we made any preparations toward that end, we were raided again on Gina's birthday. This time I was standing outside in the yard of the apartment next door. The police (a couple of guys with suits on) walked right past me and into our apartment. Realizing who they were, I quickly ran up about three steps and got in between my neighbor's screen door and the main door. Since no one was in our apartment and the door was open I think he realized that the person he had just passed was probably the person that lived there and immediately came back out to look for me. Because I was hiding between my neighbor's doors, he saw Kenny standing in the same spot where I was wearing a leather jacket and about my height. So, mistaking him for me they assumed I wasn't involved since I was still standing there.

As fate would have it, Roy, one of my young friends in the neighborhood who always shared his grass with me, had brought a young girl over to our place and got caught up in the raid. Since she was a minor that only further complicated the situation. Since I was not in the apartment at the time, I tried to head off Gina, who was coming from a class via the commuter train from downtown. Our neighbor Jennese and I were going to surprise Gina on her birthday. Well, I was unable to head her off and instead she had a horrible surprise. The police had found some grass in Kenny's room and poor Gina was charged for it. In the end she was not held responsible for what was found in our roommate's room and all charges were dropped. As it turned out, according to one of the policemen our landlord, Armstrong was responsible for the raids, attempting to make us move out. Kenny was charged with possession and his parents took care of his legal expenses. It was very clear however that we had to vacate the premises ASAP.

At this point I was still getting high a lot and I was going through a period that I wanted to forget. At some point Gina moved out, but it seemed for a very short time. When she came back, someone asked Gina if she wanted a dog. I guess we decided to check it out. Gina went out to investigate and came back with this beautiful dog. At the time, not knowing much about dogs, I didn't know what kind of dog it was. It looked and acted much like a wolf to me. As it turned out she was a Siberian Husky, slimmer and taller than most, which indicated a slight mix. I would find out later that she was almost blind, which could account for the previous owners wanting to get rid of her. By this time, I was attached to her, and she would always get compliments when I would walk her, and she was an excellent watchdog. To hasten our progress of moving, Armstrong returned Gina's last rent check saying that they didn't allow dogs in the building, and we would have to move.

It was during this period that I met Tony. Tony was a young dark-complexioned brother who had a white wife, Nancy who was the mother of his daughter. Tony was really a kid when we first met. I think we first met through Kenny. Tony and I hit it off right away for whatever reason. There were quite a few kids from a slightly younger generation who had grown up in and around Hyde Park that I hung out with due to my drug networking. Tony, young and still growing as was evident in the fact that he was a normal size kid when we met, but during the time we spent together he turn into a kind of big guy. In any case he and Nancy and Gina and I were looking for a place to stay so we all decided to get a place together, which we did. We found a place on 53rd St and Woodlawn just across the street from a place called Nicky's Pizzeria, a very popular Italian restaurant in Hyde Park at the time.

Moving into the place on 53rd St. in a way marked the beginning of the end. It was about that time when I experienced probably the saddest moment in my marriage. One night, I guess, I was supposed to meet Gina at a party. When I got there, I saw her apparently looking for me. The instant I saw her I was shocked. What I saw was a defeated woman. She had her black jacket that we both wore from time to time. She had this look as if she was trying to be tough, but she looked so defeated inside. What had happened to that beautiful, bright young woman that had stepped out of my dreams at the Natural History Museum on that Easter Sunday morning? What had she done to deserve this? All she had done was to try to spend her life with me. At that point I was not feeling like a very good human being. I wanted to grab her and hold her a long time, but I didn't want her to see herself as I saw her at that moment. The last thing she needed was for her to feel sorry for herself. When I approached her, I acted as if everything was normal, but in my heart, I was extremely saddened as it was becoming clear that her happiness might depend on her freeing herself from me. When I think of a very sad moment in our marriage, that's what I think of.

One night at the apartment something very strange happened. I was in our bedroom, Gina, Nancy, and Tony were in the living room. Gina and Nancy were talking, and Tony was sleeping on the floor. While I was in the bedroom, I had fallen asleep and was having this dream. In the dream this friend of Tony who had borrowed Tony's car had wrecked it. When he reported it to Tony, a fight ensued, and Tony was getting the worst it. Suddenly I was awakened by Tony's moans. I then heard his wife call out to him,

"Tony, wake up!", then Tony described to her the exact dream I was having, and he was moaning at the same time he was getting the worst of the altercation. It was clear to me that our minds had some strong connection at that time. The reality of that experience was undeniable.

One day I learned that Tony was arrested, convicted for burglary, and sentenced to jail. When it was time for him to serve his time, he was allowed to get on a work release program, which would allow him to be free during the day to work, as long, as he returned by a certain time each night. It would be my job to get him back to check in each night. He worked at a restaurant in a church facility which was also a hang-out for the youth in the community. It was a place where he hung out before he was busted so if I got him back to the jail on time everything was cool. It was sort of like being free, but you must go back to jail each night. We did however get through that experience.

While we were living at that apartment we had three pets, a dog and two cats. Ghanja was a cool dog that I liked a lot. When I would come home from work, she would always be excited to see me. One day when I came home, she was jumping up on me and wagging her tail. Gina made some comment suggesting that I am greeting Ghanja better than I greeted her. I then responded with a flippant remark like," When you are as glad to see me as she is, I'll greet you the same way". That was a comment I wished I hadn't made.

Tony and Nancy had a very cool Siamese cat and then a little later someone told us that a friend of theirs had a litter of kittens whose parents were show cats, but since the owners were away for an extended period, they asked their friend to give them away. When we went over to check them out, they were Tabbies and they had beautiful swirls on their sides. There was one male that was kind of energetic that seemed a little mischievous and was more aggressive in exploring me. I kelp referring to him as "that little sucker", so we brought him home and named him

"Sucker". As Sucker was growing up, the cats had this ritual in the wee hours of the night where they would play war games. They would run through the apartment, hide behind doorways jumping out and attacking, chasing each other. One image stands out in my mind. The Siamese was coming down the hall as if he were stalking a prey, and suddenly Sucker jumped out from behind the door with all four legs extended much like the flattened cat in a cartoon. The Siamese then retaliated with a few quick swipes and they both darted down the hall. It all happened in a flash, and I was impressed by their martial art skills.

It was also around this time that I began having run-ins with Pacci, a local neighborhood small gang leader. When he saw us, he would take some time out of his busy day to harass us, especially me. Looking back on it, I think Pacci saw me as an arrogant bastard who needed to be brought down a peg, and he would make sure that I knew that he was the boss in that neighborhood. One evening at some party or public gathering, he and his boys surrounded Gina and me on our bikes. I don't remember exactly what they did, but it was something like stroke her hair. A few people started gathering around almost immediately. I think they wanted me to give them any opportunity to kick my ass and humiliate Gina. I then asked why they would do that and pointed out that I would not do that to his woman.

At this point the idea of having an audience was my friend. Although I was addressing him, I was certainly talking to the audience as well. I don't think that what they were doing was going to make them more popular in the hood and I think he knew it. Although I don't really remember the conversation, he did jokingly pretend to understand what I was saying and let us go. However, one thing was certain, he was not going to allow us to win any confrontation with him. Therefore, after they left, true to form, we noticed Gina's purse was missing. Poor Gina! I felt that hanging out with me, she seemed to always get the worst of the situation, but she never complained and always seemed to hang tough. The situation could have been much worse, and if my ego had gotten the best of me, it would have been much worse.

There was one time when we were at a party at the same church with the restaurant where Tony worked, and Pacci was there. When he saw us, he stepped in front of us sort of gap-legged in an almost lewd manner. At that point I had lost my patience, and I don't really remember what I said, but in essence I told Gina I needed to step out for a few minutes. Since we lived close by, I went home and got my gun. When I returned Pacci was getting in trouble with either the police or the people who were running the event. In any case he left, and I didn't have to confront him. After thinking about it I was very glad it turned out the way it did because nothing good could have come out of that confrontation. Gina and I at this point were already at the end of our relationship and she moved out having found support in her new friend Les who worked at Enrico's Restaurant where she was working while she was in school.

I had already begun having stiffness in my right knee and at one point I had tried to ride my bike and work through it. However, that only made it worse. It was becoming apparent that my knee was degenerating, my health was declining, and Rheumatoid Arthritis was raising its ugly head throughout my body. At that time, I was still managing to stay plenty high and the sequence of events at this point was somewhat fuzzy in my memory. Of course, the depression from losing Gina and my health degeneration was making this whole period something I would like to forget. I remembered Dr. Williams, my childhood doctor saying that R.A. seemed to be tied to your overall well-being and when you were happy your health would be at its best and when you were miserable it would be at its worst.

Sometime during this period, I became mostly bedridden, my job ended, and I was receiving public aid. I was having doctor visits at the hospital next to the hospital where I had worked. The parking was quite a way from the entrance and my knee was too painful to walk that distance. So, every time I had a doctor's visit I would get a parking ticket, which I would tear up and through on the ground. I eventually acquired quite a few of tickets. At one-point Ghanja had crapped on my pillow and I beat her and tied her up on the back porch with her food. The neighbors of course complained because she was crying and howling on the back porch. After a day, maybe two days I went out there to see her, and she was completely defeated. She was lying in her own crap and showed no spirit at all. When I saw her, I felt so bad and I thought, "What am I doing?" We were both at rock bottom and I was treating her like an enemy. I felt so bad I reached down and hugged her. I cleaned her up and brought her inside. She was probably just looking for my love in the first place. She became such a good dog after that.

I remember a friend who was visiting me gave me a small plastic sandwich bag of pills, which turned out to be acid (LSD) and told me to "Just go for it." I thought at the time he meant to drown myself in the euphoria of the acid, but after thinking about it, I thought he might have been telling me to take my life. I felt that if there was any potential to have a good feeling, ever again it was worth staying alive. Although if I had been in constantly agonizing pain, I guess I would have had to rethink that.

My health hadn't been that bad since I was an adolescent, and I began thinking that even though the doctors didn't have the answer, somewhere in this big environment there had to be a solution to my health problems. The concept of mind over matter came to mind. I remember an old lady in my church when I was a kid who seemed to have confidence that she could change anything through her religion. I started reading whatever was available on prayer from different religions. What I ended up with was the possibility to change the reality of one's mind through the power of suggestion. Believing that the mind was the controlling station of the body, if I could change my mind then maybe my body would change.

I began my attempt to program my mind. I would do this through a combination of visual symbols. I burned the thought in my mind that whenever I saw a vertical line, I would become stronger. Whenever I saw a horizontal line, my music would improve. Seeing both the vertical and the horizontal lines together would improve my health. Visualizing a circle would enhance my wisdom. The infinity sign represented love and the "X" shape inside the infinity sign was for my protection. All of it combined formed what I called "My Symbol", which was basically a cross, a circle and an infinity symbol combined into one symbol. My practice consisted of meditating or intensely focusing on this symbol as much as possible, usually, morning and evening, although I did put the symbol in something like a little picture locket that I wore around my neck on a chain. I would use that little symbol from time to time throughout the day. I had never heard of a mandala before, however, that's exactly what it was. I had created a mandala.

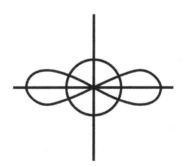

Bobby's Symbol (*I will Discuss mandala later*)

One day, my health having improved somewhat, I was hanging out in front of the apartment with Roy, my young drug buddy, and he was telling me about these Buddhists and what cool parties they had. He had these cool beads around his neck which he said were Buddhist beads. As we were talking, a very hot looking young lady with a tight blue skirt walked past us on the other side of the street. When Roy saw her, he said that she was a Buddhist. "Oh really", I said. Then I called out to her saying, "My friend said you're a Buddhist." She came across the street. When she approached, I said, "Where can I get some beads like that?" (Pointing to the beads Roy had around his neck.) To my surprise, she said," Come with me and I'll show you." Just then Gina came down the stairs from the apartment. I don't remember the exact point that Gina left me, but I think she said she came by to see how I was doing. I was still getting plenty high and all the stuff I was going through was something anyone would be trying to forget.

I was getting ready to follow the girl in the blue skirt, whose name was Jan, and I invited Gina to come along. We went to an apartment in the neighborhood where a woman gave us an application to sign to receive this scroll called a Gohonzon. I remember Gina asked me "What are we signing"?" And I said, "What can they hold us to? There's no money exchanged." In any event, Gina went on her way, and I went home. That day was August Friday the 13th 1971, a day that I have come to remember as the day of my rebirth. As I look back, that "Friday the 13th "was one of the luckiest days of my life.

That day was certainly a milestone in my life. The eight years I spent with Gina were in fact my young adult life. I could not have had a more devoted wife and lover. When we were newly-weds, I genuinely felt that no one had a more adorable and supportive wife than I had. I certainly take total responsibility for our marriage ending the way it did. I will say however, having grown to believe in karma that I do believe our purpose in life was to be fulfilled in separate paths.

Chapter III
Chicago II

NSA (Nichiren Shoshu of America)

When Gina and I signed the application for the Gohonzon we were given instructions to chant "Nam-myoho-renge-kyo" fifteen minutes in the morning and again in the evening. I did follow those instructions and since I didn't have a Gohonzon I would chant to my symbol. I remember that when I started chanting to my symbol, I experienced a slightly different feeling than I had felt before. I guess it was sort of stepping outside myself in a way. In any case, I liked it.

At one point someone had given me an address to a meeting. The meeting was located on S. Jeffery Ave., and I think the name Thomas was on the bell. I knew the block where it was supposed to be located but I had lost the exact address. It was a highly populated block and I estimated there were over a thousand apartments in that block. Well, I thought this was an opportunity to test this chant. So, I figured I would park my car wherever I could and go from building to building until I saw the name Thomas on a bell. I pulled my car into the first parking space available and started with the building closest to me. When I entered the doorway and looked on the list of names on the wall, I did see a Thomas on the listing. Of course, Thomas was a common name so there was nothing unusual about that. So, I pushed the button. I expected a voice asking for identification, but they just buzzed me in. As I opened the door and started up the stairs, I heard voices chanting "Nam-myoho-renge-kyo". When I heard that sound, I got goose bumps. The chance that the only parking space available and the first building I walked into was the right place certainly impressed me. I remembered the first time I said those words that a gorgeous woman gave me a big smile. Anyway, it seemed a little spooky to me, but in a good way. The meeting was also good. It was very high energy with singing songs about their Buddhist practice to the tune of Nat Adderley's "Work Song", a popular jazz tune at that time. People were giving experiences about things that happened when they chanted. I was kind of pumped when I left the meeting. Focusing on my symbol was never like this. The most impressive thing was theoretically they were saying things that made sense to me.

When I left that meeting, I went to spend some time with friends. I was very excited and wanted to share my experience with them. As it turned out they had taken some acid (LSD). My whirlwind type of presence had the effect of bringing them down. As a matter of fact, one of my friends (who was the same friend that had given me that bag of acid when I was lying in bed looking hopeless) later told me that my presence and high energy sort of freaked them out. At this point I had my sights on getting one of those scrolls they were chanting to.

Getting one of those scrolls (the Gohonzon) would turn out to be a little more involved than I had originally thought. At that time the Gohonzons were only issued by the priesthood, and they only came around about every six months. I would have to chant until the following February without one. I don't remember the details, and I do remember chanting to my symbol before I received my Gohonzon, but at some point, my symbol just seemed to be phased out.

NSA as an organization in Chicago at that time had a small headquarters building, the Community Center, on the north side of town. I don't remember more than three or four subdivisions called chapters and the chapters were broken down into districts. The district was the main support group for the individual in the organization. The one I practiced in was the Avalon District. Its meeting place was the same place that Gina and I had applied for a Gohonzon. I think we had district meetings once a week and the meetings certainly gave me the support, I needed to establish my practice.

Meanwhile for some reason Ghanja, my dog, Sucker, my cat, and I had to find another place to stay. I'm pretty sure Tony and Nancy wanted a place for just the two of them anyway. Believe it or not, my next apartment was in the same building where we had all the drug busts. At that point I was not feeling very secure about my circumstances and decided to get rid of everything but what I could keep in my car. I didn't have a lot anyway and when Gina and I split, we made it clean, and she took whatever she wanted. I wound up with the car and the stereo. Living off a public assistance check, I couldn't afford the apartment. So, I took on a roommate, a young student who also needed a roommate. We didn't remain roommates very long because one day he was having a few guests over when I wasn't there and Ghanja wouldn't let them in. So of course, he moved out shortly after that. I'm sure I couldn't pay a whole month's rent, so I would have to find another place. This all took place in February 1972 and that was the month I received my Gohonzon.

I received my Gohonzon on February 27th, 1972, after waiting six months for the priests to come around. There were a lot of people wanting to receive one and the small Buddhist center was too small for the ceremony. They had to rent a facility to house the activity. The ceremony consisted of all the recipients lining up and the priest would say something in Japanese and then the recipients would say, "I do. "Nowadays everything is in English, so you know what you are saying "I do" to. The priest would tap each of the recipients on the head with what I found out later was a rolled up Gohonzon. Of course, they were obviously having us pledge something and I had no fear of pledging something I didn't understand. After witnessing the excitement of those who practiced this stuff and my couple of experiences, I was chomping at the bit to get my hands on one of those Gohonzons. Just the small chance that there was something to this stuff was all I needed.

So, it was the tradition at the time to enshrine it in your altar ASAP, and a couple of young leaders (a man and woman) came to my apartment to do the job. I had set up an altar in preparation for the event, which consisted of a small piece of furniture which was basically a little box that had no front or back that I painted black to match my *butsudan,* a small housing with two doors in the front to protect the Gohonzon, which I hung on the wall over the box-like piece of furniture that held two candles, an incense burner, a small cup of water and sometimes a small piece of fruit as an offering. This was very ritualistic but typical of the Buddhist members' homes I had visited.

The enshrinement began as with every other Buddhist activity, with a recitation called *gongyo.* Gongyo, translated as "assiduous practice," was learned by all members. I was thoroughly impressed with the fact that they all learned this long, complicated portion of the Lotus Sutra which dated back to 600 to 1,000 BCE. The organization was mostly young people that were from all economic and social backgrounds. Many of these kids were teenagers and they would all recite gongyo together. At that time the format was also complicated. Some of the portions were repeated several times along with a very long portion recited once. The first time I tried to do it on my own it took me 1½ hours. Once you had learned it at the regular speed it would take about 20 minutes to ½hour. I was simply amazed that they were able to get that many people to want to do it. In any case that's what we did at my enshrinement. I was a member of NSA. Now all I had to do was learn gongyo.

Harper Court

So, of course it was time to find another place to stay. I found a place in a shopping area called Harper Court. Harper Court was very cool. It had a courtyard that descended about three feet below the sidewalk around it. It was surrounded by various types of art shops and imported goods shops. It was not unusual to find musicians giving a free concert in the courtyard. At the advice of a social worker, I had applied for disability income from the Social Security service but hadn't received anything yet. Not working, I spent a lot of time hanging out in the courtyard. There were a few other guys without jobs that would hang out there daily. All of us were making determinations of future success in between flirting with the women that might pass by. Personally, I had learned gongyo and was chanting every day and was attending Buddhist meetings one or two times a week.

My place was a one-room apartment with a tiny hallway with a closet and a bathroom as you entered the place; to your left was the main room. At the far end of the room (north end) were a set of double doors, or maybe one double door with four panels, English-style that was mostly glass with wood frames. At the northeast corner of the apartment was a tiny kitchen. To the right of the little kitchen on the east wall of the main room were double doors that housed a pull-down double bed. The English-style double doors on the north side of the apartment were overlooking 52nd street and felt like a balcony, but it was just a window ledge with a waist-high wrought iron railing.

Harper Court was a section of Harper Ave. that had been blocked off between 52nd street on the north and 53rd street on the south, originally for art shops only but had evolved by the time the project was completed. I liked the place except for one thing. Even though the stove was fully functional some previous tenant had only cleaned the surface of the stove, leaving the inside disgustingly full of grease and who knows what else. I decided I would rather eat out every day than try to tackle that. The refrigerator was fine so I would keep some food in it, but nothing I would have to cook. When I wanted hot food, I went out.

It was there that I developed a consistent practice. Every morning and evening when I would do gongyo and chant, Ghanja would lie in the middle of the floor and Sucker would sit next to me with his feet tucked in my slippers. He seemed to be more aware of what I was doing than Ghanja. When I would be chanting and get a little goosebump type of feeling, Sucker would give out a little meow at the same time. Everything was going quite smoothly except for the fact I never seemed to have enough money. The disability check, which I applied for, still hadn't come.

One day when I was very broke with less than five bucks and feeling desperate, as I was entering my building lobby, I stopped and checked the mail as I usually do and saw what looked like a check. When I opened it, it was my disability check and it had a retroactive amount of $464.00 (not sure about the exact amount), which was more than I would be getting because although I had just now received a check, they paid me from the time I first applied. When I saw the amount, it seemed familiar. I looked in my pocket and discovered that I had $4.64 in it. Of course, in looking at the money I couldn't help noticing the correlation between the two amounts.

Months later when I was broke again, I desperately went through my car and looked under and behind the seats and below the carpets and came up with $2.63 in change. Again, before I went up to my apartment, I checked my mail and it seemed to be a check in it. Now, remembering the last time I was desperately broke, I was pretty sure I knew the amount of the check. Sure enough, the check was for $263.00, 100 times the amount I had in my pocket, just as before.

It was also around this time that I had an appointment that was important to me, although I don't remember what it was for, but I had to get up at a certain time to get where I wanted to be. The next morning while I was sleeping a fly started buzzing around my head. It was very annoying and persistent. Out of frustration I swung viciously at the fly. At that moment I noticed the clock and it was exactly the time that I needed to get up. It was like the fly knew I needed to get up right then. All these events made me think back to the time at Chicago Music College when I was desperately broke, and I found a $20.00 bill. No matter how I looked at it, something that appeared bigger than me was on my side. It is true that the incident at the Chicago Music College was before I had begun practicing this teaching, but it was at CMC that I first ran into Nam-myoho-renge-kyo and the beginning of my spiritual awakening. All in all, I felt that what

I had been doing was a sincere effort to improve my life and it certainly seemed to be paying off.

Sucker and My Transitioning Into NSA

As I said before, Sucker seemed to be very much in tune with what I was doing with my practice. After I scolded him a couple times about going under my altar, he never did it again. I was away from home more than I had been since I had run into David, the same person who introduced me to Buddhism and discovered that he was the band director for a young men's group that they called the Brass Band. Since David was directing the band, I was drawn to it as they prepared for the Columbus Day Parade. I practiced with them even though I didn't think I would be able to march because of my right knee, which had been the focus of my most recent arthritis attack.

One night I had a dream. In the dream I was looking through an opened door. I saw Sucker lying there dead and behind me there were a couple of cats walking back and forth. My first thought was that the cats had killed Sucker. I woke up and was very disturbed. This happened on Friday night. I was very concerned, and I shared my dream with the people at the practice the next day, Saturday. When I got home after Sunday's practice in the afternoon, Sucker didn't come out to meet me like he and Ghanja usually did. I looked for him and discovered that he was under my altar and not looking very good.

There was an animal clinic right there in Harper Court about two doors south of my building. The next day, which was Monday, I took him to the clinic. They told me I would have to leave him there and they would call me. They did call and said he had kidney stones (or gallstones), and they would need to do surgery. Of course, I told them to do it although I didn't have a lot of money. I couldn't let him die. The next day they called me and told me Sucker didn't make it through the surgery and that I should come to the clinic. When I got to the clinic, they led me back to a room where a few cats were and opened the refrigerator door. There was my dream! Sucker lying there dead, the light coming from the other side of the door, the refrigerator door, like in my dream and the two cats walking back and forth behind me. I had just experienced seeing the future, but at the time that was overshadowed by the loss of Sucker. He was such a beautiful tabby with a big swirl pattern on his side, and he was hardly more than a kitten. I think it was that very night that I had another dream. In this dream Sucker was running in a yard as if to tell me that he was finally free from the confines of that small apartment. Ordinarily I wouldn't give that dream any special significance, but after all I had been through recently with Sucker, I took it to heart.

A while later there was young lady I had dated for a short time, who had said she was born with a veil over her face, which meant to older people in my childhood that you could see ghosts. I was kind of surprised that a young Latina would even know what that meant. Now, of course, that's something I never ever, really believed. One night while we were sitting around smoking weed, she asked me if I had a cat. I asked her why she asked. She said that she kept thinking she just saw a cat. When I asked her to describe it, she described a tabby type of cat. I showed her a picture of Sucker and asked her was this the cat? She said," Yes. Where is it?" When I told her that he had passed away she decided to leave shortly after that. All of this was certainly no proof of the validity of ghosts, but with all the experiences I had been recently experiencing, I was pretty much open for anything. After it was all done, I chanted to be responsible for Sucker's future happiness if possible.

Sucker

Ghanja and Me

Suzanne

I can't say that I had strong faith, but my confidence in this philosophy was certainly growing stronger and I was very active in the organization.

I was however a single man about 28 years old with the same drives that all young guys my age had. Since I had been in my apartment, I had only dated a couple of young women, both of whom were from the little community where I lived with Gina and the other roommates. They were younger than I was, and it was always my assumption that they were curious from watching me in that environment where I was living with three women. It was also my assumption that they both were probably disappointed after hanging out with me. One had introduced me to gay bars, which I would never have gone in on my own, but as it turned out, hanging out with the LGBT community was fun.

One of the places I would hang out was a place called The Wise Fools, a fun bar that had a separate room with tables and a bandstand. There were occasionally some pretty good groups in there, like the sons of Dave Brubeck. One night, I was at the bar, and I had just stopped smoking cigarettes for about three months and was feeling cool about my ability to drink without smoking. At that point two long-legged, long-haired women came up and sat on either side of me. One was blonde and one was a red head. As they began talking to me, they lit a cigarette and stuck it in my mouth. I had no fucking will power at all. I started smoking again right then. As it would turn out they were a couple of kids, barely drinking age, who I hung out with for a couple of days going to parties and I still hadn't gotten anywhere. So, I had to bail out.

I also used to hang out around the pool table at The Wise Fools, and that's where I ran into Suzanne. She was a regular there and I would always see her shooting pool with her hair pinned up, I imagined she did that to keep it out of her way while she was playing. She was kind of cute as she would walk around the table, talking shit to the guys and capturing a reddish tint in her hair from the overhead light, as she would lean over the pool table. I don't remember how we hooked up. I just remember us migrating toward each other and then we started hanging out at my place and sometimes at hers.

It was with Suzanne that I first experienced what I would have called a sort of mental telepathy that humans have with each other. It was doing this period when I first began chanting that I would begin noticing that when I would think of her, she would call me. Now, I'm not implying that whenever you want to get in touch with someone, that all you only need to do is chant Nam-myoho-renge-kyo. However, sometimes when I would just think of her, she would call, which was something I had not experienced before so regularly, and I attributed it to the fact that I was chanting so regularly. It is not unusual for a twin to feel anxious when the other twin is in trouble or for one to be thinking about someone and shortly thereafter run into them. Anyway, I frequently experienced things of that nature, like a little bit of mental telepathy during my Buddhist practice, more than I had experienced before I began practicing.

Suzanne was an art student at Columbia College, located near the lake (Lake Michigan) in the north side of the Loop, the downtown area in Chicago. She walked around with a little swagger, almost with a slight tough girl attitude. As it turns out she was an orphan, which might account for her seeming a little less inhibited than what I would associate with the average middle class white girl, at least at that time (early 70's). When I think of an orphan I think of Dog, the kid that I watched grow up after first seeing him in an orphan home while I was with the church group I described earlier. Dog's story was a tragic one and he never seemed to have a chance to escape his circumstances. While Suzanne, on the other hand, was going to school and coping with life in a positive way.

There was no real commitment in our relationship. We just spent our time together and were very open with each other. I still sometimes frequented the coffee shop in the church where Tony, my ex-roommate used to work. There were a lot of guys that hung around there that she used to flirt with. She complained that when she would make a pass at them, they would say, "Aren't you Bobby's girl friend?" Then she would imitate me by walking across the room with what is called the pimp walk, which was popular among young males in the Black community for as long as I can remember. It might best be described as walking with a very cool swagger, with a slight limp and swinging your arm in sync with every other step.

As she was doing the pimp walk, she would say," I'm Bobby, I've got Arthritis". That was her depiction of me. I loved her sense of humor and her carefree attitude. She was certainly streetwise, and I always felt she could fit in, in any situation. One time when my mother was coming to town, she called and asked me would I go to church with her. She knew I had recently started chanting and she was afraid I might not want to go. Well, I told her I would go and meet her there. So, wearing my super-fly suit that I had purchased at a place called Smokey Joe's, and Suzanne wearing a colorful outfit with a long skirt, we went to church to meet my mother and my stepfather who was a minister. We spent some time with them and took a few pictures. As we were leaving, my mother pulled me to the side and said to me, with a smile, that she had been worried about me since I had recently split with Gina, but her recent husband who was a minister told her not to worry because I looked like I was doing just fine.

Suzanne was dedicated to her art and was uninhibited in that area as well. At one point when she had to turn in an art project and had an idea of giving birth to the urban life, or something like that, something that she had seen an earlier artist express and she wanted to give it a shot. We went to an overpass across a major Chicago freeway during a very busy time of the day and took a photo of the oncoming traffic. She then superimposed it with a full-frontal photo of herself as if in a birthing stirrup. There she was, giving birth to the "Dan Ryan" freeway in Chicago. It certainly was an "in your face" piece. It was such a daring piece that I wasn't sure she was going to turn it in, but she did. I often wondered what kind of grade she got for that.

Once when I was attending an NSA meeting, a leader was addressing the offerings that we sometimes put on our altar and said that by offering something sincerely that you like to the Gohonzon, it come back into your life in abundance. On hearing that I offered a shot glass of reefer (marijuana) to my Gohonzon. Although, it was a halfhearted gesture, a short time later, maybe a week, I was picking Suzanne up at her school, and when she got into the car, she asked me would I like a free bag of grass? When I asked her to explain, she said someone had just offered to give her a bag of grass and would I be interested in it. So, I said sure, thinking that it would be garbage. She then ran back in and came back with a large lunch bag of weed. I was expecting her to come back with a tiny bag that they used to refer to as a nickel bag (nickel = $5.00) which is about a shot glass in quantity, but instead it was maybe a half pound, and it was decent stuff. And besides it was free. However, it caused me to think, "was this something that I wanted an abundance of in my life?" If the offering that I put on my altar could bring about such a clear-cut result, maybe I should take this a little more seriously. In any case I decided not to do it again.

One of the things we would do at the time was to frequent blues clubs. On one occasion we were at this club where a somewhat famous blues artist was performing. Suzanne left to go to the lady's room. When she returned from the lady's room, she said," I just had J.W.'s dick in my hand." I asked what the hell was she talking about. She then explained that when she went to the lady's room, which was down the stairs, she had somehow gotten lost and went into the wrong door and found herself in a room with J.W., who proceeded to make a serious advancement toward her. She said he was approaching her with all his glory exposed. She said that she grabbed his glory and then was able to finagle her way out of the door. Like I said she was streetwise and I'm sure she had been in worse situations.

One day Suzanne had invited a student from Columbia College where she was attending school. The student, Donna, was a very pretty girl with a milk chocolate complexion. Suzanne and Donna needed to connect with each other regarding some personal transaction and Donna had asked her boyfriend to escort her to my place. Apparently, Donna had some mystical connection with the use of the phrase "Nam-myoho-renge-kyo", where she had been saying those words and getting some positive results. What happened next could probably best be described from Donna's point of view as she later described it to me. She said that when she first entered my place, I was lying on the bed looking somewhat sickly and puny. Then, when Suzanne asked me to explain my practice to her, I sat up and suddenly came alive to such an extent that she said that by my actions alone she felt the power of what I was trying to say. After inviting her to a few meetings she became a lifelong Buddhist as well as a lifelong friend.

Up until then, I was still a reasonably new member of NSA. I remember on one occasion a girlfriend of Suzanne's invited us to go out on her dad's boat with her. As it turned out, there was an NSA young men's training outing scheduled at the same time we were supposed to go out on the boat. I think I had already paid a small fee to attend the training outing. Now, as I was reflecting on both activities, it was clear that I had to make a choice. Should I go on the trip with the young men or the boat with two hot girls. Although I was a new member to the NSA, I had been developing a feeling of responsibility toward the group. NSA's goal as a group was world peace through individual happiness. So, of course my rationale was that I would be a lot happier out there on that boat with the two girls than I would be on the excursion with the young men. My decision was made. I would be going with the girls.

At the time of the trip either Suzanne or her friend had scored some acid (you know, LSD). This trip was looking better by the moment. That evening we all piled into my Volvo and drove to, or near Navy Pier. We boarded the boat and proceeded to hang out and get high. I have no idea how long we were on the boat, but if my memory serves me correctly that I found a way to start irritating Suzanne, and besides that the acid didn't seem to be very good to me, so we decided to get off the boat. When we got back on the pier and went through what I think was the restaurant at Navy Pier, the acid hit me like a ton of bricks. Suddenly, I was very paranoid. My memory starts getting pretty sketchy at this point, but the next thing I remember was being in front of Suzanne's friend's place without Suzanne. We then went up to her place, but keep in mind that I was getting higher every moment. After a short time, my heart was pounding like mad, I had lost total confidence in my judgment and was pretty sure I was starting to irritate her. After a while the consensus was that I should go home. The only problem was, I had to drive home this way. Well, I did drive home and survived the evening. It is an understatement to say that the evening did not go exactly as planned. At my next NSA activity everyone was talking about the awesome activity the young men had. I did take note of that. The time I spent together with Suzanne, was reasonably short-lived. Maybe only a few months. However, the impression she made on me was much greater. One day I remember Suzanne mentioning some guy who had an antique business, who I got the impression was making a play for her. I think it was at the same time she suggested that we might move in together. I expressed that I didn't think that was a good idea at the time. As I think back on it, I think that was probably an ultimatum. I think the next time I talked to her she was in the antique business. She left my life as gracefully as she came in.

The Youth Division Band

During the early 1970's in NSA, in the Midwest Headquarters, based in Chicago, all the youth division had to be part of either the Brass Band (young men) or the Fife and Drum Corps (young women). The purpose of this was to train leaders for the future. In my opinion that concept was highly successful. The Brass Band, and the training and experiences I had with it would become a major part of my life for years to come.

As I mentioned before, I don't remember all the details of it all, but I was surprised when I found out that David, who had introduced me to this teaching, was the Brass Band leader. David and I have created quite a history together with music in NSA. My very first challenge was the Columbus Day Parade but there would be many more. When I first started out with the band, the Columbus Day Parade was the main opportunity for us to play in the community. At that time, it seemed that 90% of NSA was between their late teens and their early thirties. The other 10% were pioneers of the movement consisting of a great deal of Japanese wives and their American military husbands. Of course, this is from my point of view and not a statistic.

The ages between the late teens and the early thirties were considered youth division. Not all those youth could participate in the Brass Band or the Fife and Drum Corps. Many of these young people had considerable experience in organizing and people moving, and they were very helpful in organizing and carrying out activities on both a large and small scale. The young men's activities would be primarily outside while the young women's would be primarily inside during large activities. The organization was structured in what was called a four-divisional system which reflected the family unit (mother, father, son, and daughter) and at that time also reflected society at large since the man was usually the central figure as the father was considered the head of the household. It should be noted that this Buddhism was founded by the thirteenth century priest Nichiren, who was very clear about the equality of men and women, even though the society in America, Japan and around the world has taken considerably longer to catch up. The organization and the society have made progress in that area. On every level of the organization there was a leader for each division: Men's Division (MD), Women's Division (WD), Young Men's Division (YMD) and Young Women's Division (YWD). (There was, however, those under the age of 12 that was called at the time, junior pioneers, at least in some places.)

The brass band and the fife and drum corps proved to be very effective ways of training leaders for the NSA organization, much like the military. Inside the brass band organization, the section leaders were always changing, and the leaders in the other parts our movement were always changing as well. Some of the people you were leading today would be your leader tomorrow, thus, taking the ego out of the process and putting emphasis on the goal at hand. Over the years I had a lot of rewarding experiences with the brass band. I marched in a minimum of 13 parades that included a few Columbus Day Parades, Christmas

Parade in Detroit, Kentucky Derby Parade, Bicentennial Parade in New York, in the nation's capital where NSA displayed thousands of USA flags and a very long parade at the foot of Mount Fuji in Japan where we took home a first-place trophy (and then struggled to play our own national anthem). The brass band and the fife and drum corps were great schools for developing leaders and developing people who were very valuable human beings in our communities.

Lake Grove Chapter

NSA was certainly growing as an organization, and new chapters were being formed. Lake Grove was one of those chapters. During this expansion there was a new district formed called Hyde Park District which I had been appointed the leader of. Now, I certainly had never thought of myself as any kind of leader but there was a reason I had been appointed. By this time, I was excited about the practice and I as a matter of course told all my closest friends about this teaching, which included Tony, my ex-roommate, his wife Nancy, Denver, my old classmate from the Art Institute, his wife Ronnye (Veronica) and Donna, the friend of Suzanne. It was a small district but was large enough to have two groups (subdivisions of the district). Tony and Denver were Men's Division group leaders, but their wives who were Women's Division group leaders were doing most of the work keeping the district together. Donna was away most of the time becoming an Airline Stewardess that at the time was a very sought-after job by many young women. She had some serious health issues that were not noticeable to most people but would probably be an obstacle to landing that job. She chanted sincerely to land the job anyway, which she did and considered that to be one of her first major benefits of her newly found philosophy.

While in Lake Grove Chapter I experienced a lot of growth in this organization. Up until then I still hadn't been working. Occasionally I would pick up a gig with my conga drums but that was not very often. My health had improved, and I didn't like all the hoops one had to go through to get that free money. Looking back, I had become a lot more motivated and wanted to start leading a more responsible life. However, it was not that easy to find a job.

It was at this point that I decided to chant a million daimoku" The word daimoku is a Japanese word for prayer. One daimoku was saying Nam-myoho-renge-kyo once. I had been told that if you wanted to break through a difficult situation, chanting one million daimoku was a good way to do it. I had figured out that if I chanted for three hours a day, I could chant 1,000,000 in three months. This was an awakening experience. I would attend NSA activities just about every day, where I would chant. When I would come home, I would subtract whatever amount I had chanted at the activities and then complete the rest when I got home. I would sit in front of my altar and shake a few sticks of incense out of a paper cylinder into my hand to burn one stick at a time while I finished chanting.

After a while I noticed that the number of pieces of incense that would fall into my hand would always be the right amount to complete my chanting. Even when I would try to figure the amount I needed, my figuring might be wrong but the pieces that fell into my hand were always right. It was almost as if a higher consciousness was toying with me. Another thing that happened was, after being warned that things might happen to try to discourage me, I had car troubles every day for a short period of time. I knew I needed a new car and most of the problems were mechanical, but at least one time someone just backed into my headlight. The point is that I was way more aware of my surroundings than I had been. I did, however, complete my million daimoku.

It was during the winter months, and I was still looking for work. At one point I had the flu with a fever while there was a harsh blizzard outside. There was a new leader who had just tak-

103

en over the Chicago area who had come from Washington, DC. Mr. Osaki, who made a big impression on me. I had heard that he had given up the opportunity to become the first Japanese American General in the USA military to become a leader in NSA. I thought he was very cool. I liked the way he dressed and the way he carried himself and I had a lot of confidence in his opinion. I called Mr. Osaki and told him I had completed 1,000,000 daimoku and explained my situation with the weather and my health and that I needed a job. He was very strict. He asked me if I was going to lie there and die? He told me I did have a job. He said that my job was looking for work. He said I had chanted and that I should step out on a limb with this teaching. He said I should spend eight hours looking for work and take a lunch in the middle of the day like everyone else. I began looking that day. Shortly after that I did find a job, but I had a sore throat that lasted about 3 months after starting to look for it. I had been looking for a while with no real results when I decided that during the next interview I had, I would introduce the interviewer to Buddhism. The very next interview I had I did just that. During the interview I was asked by the Vice President of the company a few questions that he felt were important to him. After answering his questions, I told him that in my Buddhist practice my home life, my job and my faith activities are all one and the same and there was never an excuse to give less than 100% in either arena. Satisfied with my answers, he hired me and then said, "If all Buddhists have that attitude, the next time I put an ad in the paper it will read, 'Must be Buddhist.'"

After landing the job at *Rapid Circular Press*, I notified Social Security Disability to let them know I had begun to work again. At that time NSA was planning a big convention at the head temple in Japan. Although my financial status was quite shaky, I was encouraged to chant to go. Of course, having nothing to lose, I did just that. As it turned out there was an overlap in income. When I got what I thought was my last disability check I put it down on the trip to Japan. I think I got two more disability checks after I began working, and I had determined, after I paid for my trip to Japan, that the next check I would get would go toward a massive celebration. That check never came, but I did get to go to Japan.

Lorenzo's degeneration

It was around this period that I ran into Lorenzo again. He had returned from Vietnam. Of course, it was great to see him again, but soon after we had spent a little time together and smoked a little grass, I realized he was having some trouble perceiving reality. One day while he was visiting me, he volunteered to walk Ghanja, since I was busy doing something else. I thanked him and told him to make sure to keep her on the leash since there was a lot of traffic out there and Ghanja didn't see very well anyway. When they came back, they seemed to both be in a state of disarray. I asked what was wrong and Lorenzo said Ghanja had been hit by a car. When I examined her, she appeared okay physically. I asked. "Wasn't she on the leash?" He said that she appeared so calm that he thought she would be okay without it. He crashed at my house for a couple of days. After seeing no end to his visit, I asked him to leave.

I later heard that one evening while he was in the vicinity of his mother's house (after his father had passed away), a neighbor called the authorities on him thinking he was a vagrant. Apparently, the police had gotten a tip that he had entered this house (his mother's house). When the police went to retrieve the vagrant (Lorenzo), a fight pursued. In the fight Lorenzo overpowered one officer, took his gun, and shot and killed the other officer. I don't know the accuracy of this story, but it was my understanding that he was put away in a mental institution possibly for life. That was the last I heard of the story. Their family was such an upstanding family in the community. The father was considered an innovator of African studies in our country, the mother was also an educator (I think) and the two sons, to all appearances, had a very bright future. Lorenzo appeared to have a bright future as an artist and his younger brother seemed to be the golden boy of the freshmen in college studying philosophy. As a freshman, he had taken acid (LSD) and, at least during the time I was aware of him, never seemed to completely recover from what was an apparently "bad trip". Theirs was a tragic family story.

All the experiences I had been having were motivation to develop a consistent practice with this Buddhism. As I had mentioned, I had been practicing with David and the band, preparing for the Columbus Day parade. However, I didn't have confidence that I would be able to march in a parade because of the recent flare-up I had in my knee due to my rheumatoid arthritis). So, I decided to chant to be able to march in the parade. In discussing it with some NSA members, I had been told not to be discouraged if things got worse before they got better. They mentioned a Japanese term called *sansho shima* which translated as "Three Obstacles and Four Devils. The point was that whenever you decided to move in a good direction, negativity would surely arise to discourage you.

At the beginning of my determination on the way from my car to my apartment, I fell on my bad knee. I don't know if I had really bought in to the idea of *sansho shima,* but I certainly did think about it. I took it so seriously that I went into my apartment and chanted for two hours about it. In any case, when the parade came around, I did march, and it was much easier than I thought it would be and I was extremely excited about marching in the parade. I certainly wouldn't say that it was a miracle but it sure was a fun and exciting experience and I was extremely encouraged.

Finding a Home for Ghanja

At this point my NSA activities made it very difficult to take care of my dog Ghanja, who had become such a loyal and protective companion. I remember one night I was sitting in my car with the engine running when someone knocked on the window. When I looked, it was my old nemesis, Pacci. Ghanja sprang out of the back seat and was snarling and growling trying to get through the window. Pacci was backing up as he was gesturing "Never mind" and his entourage of friends were bent over laughing.

There was a young woman about 18 or 19 at the most, that I had gone out with a few times, who was very pretty and poised. Her home environment was one I thought Ghanja would be happy in, since there were young people, other pets and not a lot of tension that I knew of, so, I gave Ghanja to them. The downside of that was, I heard later that Ghanja had killed a newly born kitten and they had to give her up. I always regretted that I didn't make it clear that I would take her back if there were ever any issues.

Tozan – *My first pilgrimage*
Tozan was the Japanese name for our pilgrimage to the Head Temple in Japan. After living on public aid and disability income the idea of going to Japan was beyond my wildest dreams. There were a considerable number of participants from the US attending that convention in Japan, representatives from most of our major cities. All the participants would be dressed in blue business suits; not dark blue but rather more of a cyan. The women would have skirts and the men wore pants, but they were all the same color. They were uniforms much like the schools in Japan. Some of those people were wealthier than others, but the uniforms were the great equalizers.

With my experience with African drumming and the Brass Band, I had imagined a drum corps where some of the more advance drummers would step forward and take solos in dynamic fashion. When we first arrived at the temple grounds, we were greeted with a drum corps of young Japanese girls who did exactly what I had imagined but more dynamically than I had imagined. After a long grueling trip, it was much like Dorothy from "the Wizard of Oz walking out of her crashed house into this beautiful land being greeted by all the Munchkins. The young girls were so beautiful and so confident, like a dream.

We were all treated like honored guests. We were chauffeured around and cheered everywhere we went. We were all young people from different countries who had not paid a lot of money but who had to be housed and fed. We slept in these buildings called *sobos* which I can only describe as large gymnasium-type buildings that would facilitate many sleeping mats on the floor. All the US participants were divided into small groups with a translator for each group with a full agenda, i.e., meetings, conferences, meals, entertainment etc. For daily orientation, meals and bunking we would join the people in our *sobo*. For other activities in the community, we would split off into small groups with our translators. For our free time we could just explore the temple grounds, which had a lot of history, or shop at the shops which were mainly in one area of the grounds.

One day while my friend David and I were exploring this extremely peaceful and exotic environment, we ran into the famous jazz musician, Herbie Hancock. Now, David and I, who both played saxophones, were very stoked to run into Herbie. While we were introducing ourselves, David told him we were the gladiators from Chicago. David had a different kind of personality; you were never sure whether he was yanking your chain or whether he really believed what he was saying. Mostly he was just yanking your chain. When I mentioned to Herbie that I was a District Leader in Hyde Park, he told me that his mother lived in Hyde Park, and he was interested in finding a meeting place for her to attend. So, I gave him my contact info and later with the help of Veronica (Ronnye), he did connect his mom with our district. Later he came to my place during one of the meetings to check on her, however, I was not there at the time due to work.

The day came when all the visiting members would get the chance to meet President Ikeda. Now, Daisaku Ikeda was the third president of the Soka Gakkai or Value Creation Society. Although I didn't know it at the time, the Soka Gakkai was the organization that made it possible for so many people in our society to practice Nichiren Buddhism and President Ikeda was the one person most responsible for that movement. Everyone came onto the grounds to meet him. I remember it was so crowded I could not get close to him, so I climbed some stairs in a tower to see him from a distance. When he noticed that some people had climbed up the tower to see him, he gave instructions that they should come down from the tower. I felt personally crushed and even got a little teary-eyed.

I later looked at that as a lesson in the relationship of mentor and disciple. The disciple should not stand back and praise the mentor as if the mentor is a celebrity, but rather he should put forth effort to become one with the mentor toward a common goal. In this case the goal of *kosen-rufu* (World Peace). On another occasion while I was there, he was visiting the grounds again and I was able to get closer to him. As he was coming toward me, shaking hands with a long line of members, mostly women, the members would have an emotional response as he shook their hands. The women mostly would cry, and the men would also have an emotionally happy greeting. Behind him was a line of people with an emotional release while in front of him was a line of people waiting in anticipation. It was quite an image. When he got to me, he shook my hand while he was greeting someone behind me that he seemed to recognize. He never looked in my eyes. I thought about that a lot after the fact. I had no understanding and very little faith in this Buddhism and with the things that were on my mind, I wasn't sure I wanted him to look into my eyes. I was always glad, however, that I was able to shake his hand.

Going into local members' homes was a very rewarding experience. On one occasion I went to a dinner in a family's home.

Inside Sho Hondo

Everything was very beautiful and formally Japanese style. Of course, everyone squattd around the Japanese table with a nice bowl and fancy lacquered chopsticks. One of the dishes was boiled eggs that had been removed from their eggshells. Everyone would reach over and grab an egg with their chopsticks and place it in their bowl. When it was my turn to pick up my egg, the egg kept slipping from my chopsticks. As I tried two or three times, everyone looked at me with intensity as if they wanted to help but didn't want to embarrass me. I then took a chopstick and stuck it into the egg to put it in my bowl. At that instant they all broke out laughing. Problem solved.

The main purpose for going to Japan was to see the Dai-Gohonzon (Great Object of Respect, / the *Great Mandala*. Nichiren, the founder of this Buddhism, who first chanted Nam-myoho-renge-kyo on April 28, 1253, was believed to have inscribed the Dai-Gohonzon on October 12, 1279, for all mankind after inscribing several personal Gohonzons for individual members who had demonstrated strong faith. A grand temple was to be constructed with a target of 700 years from the day he inscribed the Dai Gohonzon, which would be its final resting place, but was completed in 1972 (one year prior to my visit there). This Grand Temple was called the Sho Hondo.

Sho Hondo

The Sho Hondo was built with the goal of lasting for a minimum of 500 years. Eight million lay believers, mostly Soka Gakkai members, donated more than $100,000,000 to build it, and the money was collected in an extremely short time. The main auditorium area had a roof with an impressive shape that, I was told, was influenced by the flight of the crane. The main auditorium also seated 6,600 and at the time of construction it was the world's biggest one-floor auditorium. It was constructed of the finest materials available including the finest marble. This was all placed delightfully at the foot of Mt. Fuji. The structure had acquired accolades from around the world.

The day came when we would be able to see the Dai Gohonzon. The experience was every bit as impressive as I had imagined. Everyone was lined up, I guess according to the area that they were from, and then filed into their section to take their seats. Then, on the altar stage, there were four sets of doors, two sets of electronic doors and then two on the *butsudan*, the housing for the Gohonzon). A priest would open the last two and on the final set he would seem to open very quickly as if to create maximum effect. The *butsudan* and everything surrounding it was gold, and with my Christian background I could only describe it as a little piece of heaven.

Well, we also had a parade to do. There was more than one parade and the one we participated in was the longest parade I have ever marched in, in my entire life. We marched over hills, through valleys and through narrow crowded streets. I thought it would never end.

When the parade did end all the bands gathered in this big parking lot-type area and stayed in position until all the other bands were gathered in the lot. We were standing next to a band of young Japanese girls. As we were standing in position I noticed our bass drummer, a large athletic young man who had some boxing experience, set his drum down and was leaning on it. Looking just past him I saw small young Japanese girl that couldn't be more than 14 years old standing very erect with a much bigger bass drum strapped across her chest. I wish I had had a camera to capture that image of the big guy leaning on the smaller drum while the little, young girl stood so erect with the bigger one. It was quite a contrast. I guess they had considerably more discipline that we did.

Before we left the temple grounds, we had an opportunity to see the Dai Gohonzon one more time. We were told that it was rare to see the Dai Gohonzon two times in the same visit to the temple grounds.

I'm not sure how long we were there, but I think it was somewhere between five to ten days. On the evening before the day we departed, there was a celebration, and we got a chance to learn a little bit about Japanese dancing. At one point while we were doing sort of a chorus line dance where you would have your arms around the shoulders of the persons on either side of you and kick up your leg, this young girl next to me kept closing her eyes while rubbing the side of her face on my hand. It was quite the turn-on but when the dancing was over, she was gone and there was not a chance in hell that I was going to separate from the group to try and find her.

The flight back, although long, was quite uneventful. The next thing that impressed me was the landing in the US. When I got off the plane at the L.A. airport, I could feel the tension in the air in a very intimidating way. I could feel the tension in my pores. It reminded me of the time when Gina and I were leaving Fee and Margie's place on our way to my apartment. When I walked outside the feeling of tension was very thick and in a matter of a few blocks we saw two or three fights. This was the second time I felt such an intense feeling of human anger. I think what made this feeling so prevalent was the contrast to the experience I had just had while I was in Japan.

Barbara Julia Hannum

Barbara was the oldest of my two half-sisters, Barbara and Jewel were my dad's daughters from a previous marriage, which in and of itself was not necessarily the most ideal scenario for one big happy family. However, Barbara was not typical in any way. She had a big personality with what I perceived as a lot of confidence. As far back as I can remember she used to drop by and visit us when I and my maternal siblings were all little kids. I personally loved it when she would drop in. You might make the case that I had a kid's crush on my big sister.

She was a good student in school and graduated from Knoxville College, the only Black college in Knoxville at the time and graduated Magna cum Laude in 1949. She must have started working right away after finishing school because it seemed to me that she was driving a new Chevy convertible about 1950 or '51.

As I grew older, I didn't see her so much. One day while I was living in Chicago, I think around the late '60s, I received a phone call from her, telling me that she was in town and identified where she was staying and said she would love to see me. I felt the same way and I went to the hotel as soon as I could. When I got to the hotel, she introduced to an older man who turned out to be a minister. This man did not look like any of the men I had seen Barbara date. As I was growing older it seemed to me that the older Barbara got, the younger the men that she dated. This guy was different. He was talking about his congregation in a very demeaning way, even making fun of them for being so gullible.

In my mind this was a despicable human being. However, it was still great to see my sister, who I hadn't seen in years. As it turns out that would be the last time, I would see her. Someone sent me an article about a schoolteacher in California who killed another schoolteacher by pouring acid on her face for having an affair with her son. The victim was Barbara. I thought about that a lot. I don't know the details, and I always assumed that it was in high school and the other teacher's son was probably a student. As a young adult I really took seriously the concept of karma or "What goes around comes around," but I, myself have done enough for something like that to have happened to me, for example my first wife, responding to some of my shenanigans. The year of Barbara's passing was 1973 and there will always be a special place in my heart for her.

Rapid Circular Press

In October 1973 I had worked at Rapid Circular Press for a few months. George, the owner, and boss was like a drill sergeant, a real hard ass. He was the kind of guy that would get up in your face and yell at you. Normally it didn't bother me but sometimes it would get to me. I remember on one occasion while he was in my face and I was observing his veins popping out on his forehead, I was thinking he might just blow a gasket. He then looked at me and said, "you're looking at me as if you want to say, fuck you." He was correct. A memorable moment was the time when I had lost patience with him, and as I turned to him, looking directly in his eyes, fully prepared to give up my job, and as I was about to speak, something very profound happened.

I had been practicing Buddhism for a couple of years and had learned to look at life and the universe as an infinitely compassionate and powerful existence that both me and George were part of. I had come to believe in the strict law of cause and effect and that the present moment was one of my own makings, with the understanding that the cause I was about to make would determine my future. So, when I looked into George's eyes I saw, not George, but rather the eyes of the universe looking back at me saying, "Okay, the ball is in your court." Instead of saying, "Fuck you George,", a tear rolled down my cheek. He then looked at me and said, "Bobby it's really not that serious." At that point, I just had to chuckle. He had no idea where I was coming from.

When I first started working there, I was on the night shift. All the office personal worked during the day and only me and about two or three pressmen worked at night. Since I was responsible for supplying the pressmen with their work, I had to be there until they had everything they needed. All the circulars, newspaper ad inserts, were then distributed to the newsstands when the newspapers would hit the streets. There was really no job for me during the day, which I desperately wanted and chanted for. When I came back from Japan, almost immediately they decided to cut out the night shift all together, and I began working days. Of course, to me that was no coincidence. The vice president of the company, who was also the one who hired me, left the company while I was there. He seemed always to be impressed with my Buddhist practice and before he left, he came to me and asked me to write down the words of the chant, Nam-myoho-renge-kyo.

Then there was Bob. Bob was about 50 years old or so

and had obviously not spent a lot of time around Black folks. He never passed up an opportunity to tell a racial joke. Every morning when he would clock in, he would be in a bad mood. I would always greet him from across the room with an energetic, "Good morning, Bob." His response was usually a grunt. While I worked there that was the extent of our relationship. On the day I finally left RCP, Bob approached me and invited me out for a drink. We both got a little drunk, but he was a perfect gentleman that evening. I think that is an example of how going high in response to someone going low can pay off. I was never threatened by him, and really, I think that since I was the only Black person that worked there, singling me out was his chance of not being the low man on the totem pole. I guess many people might have taken a "Fuck Bob" attitude, but I'm glad I did not.

I don't think there were more than 15 employees in the company, and I was the resident Buddhist. I didn't talk much about it on the job but sometimes I felt the other employees looked at it like some type of witchcraft. There was one instance when some of the personnel had gotten excited about doing a check pool. I think everyone would put a few bucks in a pot and the check numbers of everyone's checks would somehow be used like a poker hand. When they asked me to join their first pool, thinking that it sounded like fun, I got in. Well, as luck would have it, I won the first pool. After receiving one or two congratulations, I never heard anything else about doing another check pool; to my knowledge, there is no statistic that indicates that Buddhists win more cash prizes that anyone else. The purpose of Buddhism is to acquire absolute happiness through creating value in one's daily life and never being defeated by any obstacle. But, somehow, I don't think that explaining it, at that time would have made any difference. But, then again, maybe it would have.

There was one experience I had that would be a good example of my Buddhist practice. One day when I was still working nights, I was leaving the building. I was going through these double doors that would exit the building, not realizing that someone had locked the outside door. When I tried to go back inside that door was also locked. I realized I was stuck between the doors. I tried knocking on the inside door to get someone to bring out a key so I could leave, but it was impossible to be heard. At that point I started chanting, feeling confident that there was a solution to this dilemma. There was a bell outside the main door, but since I couldn't get out, I couldn't ring the bell. It was dark and no one was on the street, and I could be there for hours. While chanting and looking around, I noticed two tiny, covered wires that were hidden in the shadow of the doorframe and disappeared into the wall. The wires were obviously connected to a button outside the door that would ring the doorbell. I took a key and scraped the rubber off the wires just enough to be able to lay the key across the wires and make contact of the positive wire to the negative wire and ring the bell. When they came and let me free, I felt pretty good about myself and my Buddhist practice.

The greatest memories I had at RCP were with Harry. I guess the work had picked up and they hired an assistant for me. When George introduced Harry to me, he explained that Harry had worked at one job for over thirty years (which I think was a printing company), and the opportunity had come to an end, and he would be working with us. Harry was a tall, Italian gentleman, in his 60s just about ready to retire. When we met, I told him I had been married to an Italian woman and explained that the only Italian I knew was related to food. Of course, with Harry the only Italian I learned were curse words although he had a great singing voice, which was big and full, and I sometimes wondered why he couldn't have put that voice to good use.

Since Harry was twice my age, he always called me Son, and I related to that since I hadn't had a father after six years old. Harry didn't have any kids. He told me that his wife who he had been with since they were both young was disabled and he felt that the purpose of his life was to take care of her. I never met her, but I have this image of her that I think is based on a photo he showed me of her when she was younger. My image of her was a very young woman with dark, almost shoulder length, hair, reminding me of women from the 40s.

One morning Harry came in with a toothache and was carrying a little bottle of vodka to put on the tooth for pain. When we had our coffee break in the morning, he spiked our coffee with the vodka. And that was the beginning of a tradition. Every morning we'd spike our coffee, every afternoon's break we'd spike our "Bubble Up." We later started going out to lunch and having a Bloody Mary with a celery stick and Tabasco sauce. On Wednesdays, a bar a few doors down from the shop would have girls modeling bikinis, and on Fridays they would have free smelt. Hanging with Harry made it a real pleasure to come to work.

One evening after work Harry and I were at the bar, and they were raffling off a big glass punch bowl with matching glass cups. Harry was impressed with the set and I'm sure he would have used them. When they did the drawing, I chanted very sincerely for Harry to win the set. When they called the number, it was my number. When they gave me the set, I told Harry that I had chanted for him to win, but when I won, it was even better because I felt I was rewarded for my compassion, and he would get the set anyway. After I left RCP, Harry later came to my wedding and that was the last time I saw him. A few years later I called Harry after his wife had passed away, and that was the last we spoke.

I worked at RCP for about four years, and during that time I think NSA had conventions, every year. Unfortunately, the conventions did not always come at the most convenient time to take off from work. On one occasion, and I don't remember which one, I asked to take off and George said that it wasn't a good time. I told him that this time was critical. He said every time you go it's always critical so this time, I have to say "No." I then said, "I certainly understand, but I really do have to go, and

I hope I still have a job when I get back." Now, you must understand that although I did treasure my job, but with all the things I had experienced since I had been practicing this Buddhism, I was willing to give up my job and take the chance that things would work out.

When I got back my timecard was not in the card rack. Harry told me that George had hired someone to take my place, but the man that he had hired had gotten upset with George and walked off the job. So, I went into the office and got a card and clocked in. George did not pay me for that vacation time. He was a bully, but he did pay me well and showed me respect that he didn't show everyone, much to the chagrin of a few other employees. The day I finally left to go work at another company he gave me that back vacation pay. One of the times that stand out in my mind was when he and I disagreed on something and in finding out that I was right, he said to me," Well, you're right, but I will have it in for you the rest of the week." One day after I had left RCP I came back to visit, and when I went in the office to see George, he jumped up and ran across the room toward me in a mock attack and fell over some chairs. We both chuckled, and that was the last time I saw George.

Hyde Park District

After returning from Japan, I experienced a lot of growth in Hyde Park District. The women, led by Ronnye (short for Veronica) and Nancy were growing. Ronnye was a manager at a bank and at least two other women from the bank had joined our movement. She had also contacted Herbie Hancock's mother who was practicing with us. Mostly women were attending our meetings. I became so concerned about the lack of men that I went to get guidance from Mr. Osaki. When I told him of my dilemma, he simply laughed. He told me that women had stronger faith than men did and that if there were a lot of women, men certainly would come. In the long run that would prove to be correct.

Herbie came to our meeting to check on his mom although I missed him because I was working late. We even had a couple of police come by from time to time. Our district consisted mostly of young women who were outgoing, and that was obviously a winning formula. One time when I finished leading chanting at the beginning of a meeting, I turned to face the members, and to my surprise I saw Pacci, my old nemesis. After the meeting I gave him a lift somewhere and when we got out of the car an old, tattered gentleman ran up to ask for some change. Pacci jumped in front of him and chased him away. This all was a major lesson in Buddhism. Buddhism contends that the way to change your environment was for you to change first. It wasn't that long ago when the police were raiding my house or arresting me or my wife. Now they were visiting my place and offering their protection. And then, Pacci who would harass me for kicks was now my protector. It seemed to me that things around me had changed, and they had. However, ultimately, I was the one who had changed, and my environment, was simply a reflection of that change.

BBJ

Then there was BBJ -- Bobby's Bad Judgment. Although she had been around, one of the first conscious memories of her was the night a couple of well-dressed young Black men came to our meeting. Showing some interest in our meeting they invited me to a nearby restaurant to talk after the meeting. While we were at the restaurant BBJ happened to stop by and joined us for a few minutes. When she left, she gave me a light kiss on the lips and then walked away. I should point out that at that time and place it was not unusual for the people in my social circle to kiss on or near the lips when we would greet one another.

After she left however, one of the young men asked me why I would kiss a white woman like that. So, I told him that I considered all the people in the district my family and I didn't make any racial distinction between them. The two men were from a group that did distinguish racially and did not speak very highly of white people in general. After a somewhat short dialogue, I never saw them again.

It was, however, about that time that BBJ made a pass at me which I took in jest and replied, "Not in this lifetime." Little did I know at the time, she was serious, and that my comment just made her more determined to pursue me. Although I had never really noticed her closely before, she did have long wavy hair, long legs usually wrapped in tight blue jeans, with a slight thigh gap, a slight over-bite, and a sort of child-like way of expressing herself. All of which was a turn-on. I remember one time there was a major blizzard, I got a phone call from her, and she asked was I going to work. When I said no. She replied," I'll be right over," then hung up. And she came over, which was the kiss of death. Now, I knew that having that kind of relationship with your members was not good, but I was now out of control.

Then as we were talking one time, she mentioned her husband and I knew I was in over my head. One rainy evening she called me and asked could I pick her up. It was clear to me that wasn't a good idea, but, being driven by what Buddhism calls the world of rapture, I left to get her. As I walked to the car it started pouring rain, and the closer I got to the car, the harder the rain fell. When I drove off it got much worse and as I was getting closer to where she was, gusts of wind would come suddenly and shake the car while the visibility was almost nonexistent. Clearly, I was feeling like I had pissed off the Universe. When I saw her, the rain eased up and she got in the car. Although the rain had slowed down, she was like an emotional whirlwind.

After she had her way with me, I took her back to where I had picked her up and then drove home. That night was one that I reflected on many times and became thoroughly convinced that the protective universal forces were trying to protect me from

121

getting in deeper than I already was. Eventually, she told me that her husband had a fatal illness. She also mentioned that he was Black. Now, I grew up in the south when Black people were legally treated less than human. There was no way that I could feel anything less than having stabbed my own brother in the back. I was not feeling very good about myself. It couldn't get any worse than this, but it did.

One day when I was at the NSA community center, Mr. Wright, who was the central figure of the South Chicago region (at that time I think they called it a General Chapter) of NSA asked me could he speak to me for a minute. Mr. Wright was a tall Black man with a big personality who everyone loved and respected. We walked into a room, and he turned and locked the door. Mr. Wright, who always had a big smile, was not smiling. He told me that he knew what I had been doing and it had to stop. I was about 5'6" at 125lb and next to Mr. Wright I looked like a kid. His persona was even bigger than his physical size. He told me that BBJ herself had been telling people everything and if I wanted to continue to be an NSA leader, I had to stop it immediately. I told him I would take care of it.

Donna, who had fulfilled her dream as an airline stewardess was unable to attend most meetings but was introducing people to the practice and they were continuing to practice. I had been trying to encourage her to chant more and I had suggested that she should chant one whole hour at one time. One afternoon she took on the challenge. That same afternoon BBJ came by my place. I immediately told her that we couldn't see each other anymore. Of course, she always accused me of getting it on with her for a few minutes and then complaining about it for the rest of the time we were together. And she was kind of right about that. She assumed that this was one of my complaining moods. She hung around with small talk and then would try to seduce me. At one point she decided to show me her suntan lines by pulling up her top and exposing her breasts.

At this point I was starting to cave, so I looked at the clock to hurry her along. The clock said 3:15pm and I said I needed to get going. Disappointed, she hung out for a few minutes and then left abruptly. I don't remember whether I called Donna, or she called me, but when we talked, she told me enthusiastically, that she had done it. She had chanted one whole hour at one time. But then, she said, "It got really difficult at about 3:15pm." That was encouraging to me on so many levels. I really felt that if we both had lost our battles, I would have taken no less than 100% responsibility for both of us failing. But we both won and because it happened the way it did, I knew we had both achieved a milestone. Since that time all our leaders are required to sign a leadership conduct agreement which I have signed many times and always adhered to.

Supporting the Young Men
Hyde Park District was part of Lake Grove Chapter. I remember one day when I was at the NSA community center, my men's division chapter leader, Renée, was talking to Mr. Osaki in a meeting. I was in the hall, but I heard Renée mention my name. I stopped to listen. Renée was recommending me for the young men's leader for Lake Grove Chapter. Mr. Osaki, on the other hand, didn't seem to be that excited about the idea. After Mr. Osaki asked him a few questions, Renée without wavering, said I was still his choice. So, Mr. Osaki agreed to give the idea a shot. So, now I had dual positions, one as a men's division district leader and the other as a YMD chapter leader. Home visitations with members were emphasized a lot at the time and still are emphasized in our movement I took a list of young men's contact info and proceeded to contact them and set up home visitations. I did it on a Saturday and I found five young men who were willing to let me come to visit them that day. My deepest apologies for not remembering all their names, so, I won't use any of their names. They lived all over the city. One lived in a north suburb

of Chicago, a young drummer who I had heard of, and became close to. One of the young men lived way out on the south side of the city and the others somewhere in between. I visited all five young men and really enjoyed meeting them all. I had held a couple of chapter level YMD meetings, but only two or three young men had attended. After visiting these young men, they all showed up at our next chapter YMD meeting. These five young men all became the young men's leaders in their districts.

Allow me to share an experience of a young man from New York. He was visiting Chicago and apparently, someone in New York had introduced him to NSA. Since he was visiting Chicago, he connected with some NSA members. He needed a ride to the Community Center for some meeting. It was a Sunday with a lot of snow and harsh weather, and I offered to give him a ride. I picked him up and then had to pick up a couple of women. After we had everyone packed into the car, I was supposed to proceed to the Community Center where the meeting would be taking place. However, after everyone was loaded into the car, the car would not start. Anxious to get everyone to the meeting on time, I flagged down a taxi. To save money we took the taxi to the elevated train. When we got to the train station and went up the stairs to the train, the timing was perfect. Without hesitation, we walked up the steps and right into the train. Then, we had two more connections to make. When we got to the station to connect with the other train it was also right there with the door open. Again, perfect timing.

Keep in mind that all along I was quietly chanting to myself, and the young man was watching me the whole time. The women occupied themselves with conversation, obviously trusting that things would work out. He on the other hand was watching me intensely as I was chanting under my breath to make this all work out. We had one more connection to make. When we got off the train, we had to make a connection with a bus. And when we walked out to the point where the bus comes, there was no bus.

Keep in mind, I'm still chanting. However, when we arrived there and saw no bus the young man turned to me and said, "Now what are you going to do, Bobby"? I looked at him for a second, and without saying a word, I continued to chant. Just then a car drove up and someone inside the car recognized us, and said "Are you guys going to the Community Center?" We said "Yes, thank you very much." I think that answered his question. Chanting works! I don't know where that young man is today, but the last time I saw him he was still practicing in NSA.

Hawaii Convention

In the first ten years of my practice in NSA we seemed to have conventions almost every year. One of those conventions was in Hawaii where NSA built an island for a stage with a volcano right off the Waikiki beach. The volcano was set to erupt at the end of the convention during the finale. At the Hawaii convention I took on a different roll than was normal for me in the young men's activities. Normally I was mostly practicing and performing with the band. In Honolulu, however I was in the control center almost the entire time and on traffic control duty during the performances, which took place on the stage at Waikiki beach. On this trip I assisted Jesse Henderson, a more experienced young men's leader in escorting 100 young women members) on a flight from Chicago to Honolulu. The young women, most of whose ages ranged from late teens to their early thirties were performers in a fife and drum corps which created quite a lot of attention wherever we were.

Although, I did help create some music for one of the performances on the stage of this island, when I arrived in Hawaii, my activities were mainly people-moving and doing work in the control center of the convention. In doing so, I really developed more responsibility for the administrative side of being a leader in NSA. That was a major change in my life at the time. When I returned to Chicago from the convention, I became the Midwest coordinator for the brass band, which allowed me to communicate with band members in other states in the Midwest, like Minnesota, Wisconsin, Michigan, Kentucky, and Tennessee. This was all a great experience for me as a young man and I enjoyed it immensely.

Taking on Chapter level position and meeting Mildred

NSA was a young organization and in many cases an individual in their 30s and younger might take on dual leadership. For example, in my case while I was in the young men's division as a chapter leader, I was also a vice chapter leader of the men's division in Lake Grove Chapter and still District Leader for Hyde Park District.

At this point we were moving in the direction of localization in an effort, to establish district meetings closer to where the members' homes were. Since Hyde Park district was one of the largest districts in Lake Grove chapter, I was making a big effort to organize members in certain areas and creating meeting places close to their homes. At that time, I was certainly not computer savvy and did everything the old-fashioned way, which was taking a big map and locating members' homes on it to determine where their group meetings could be held. After evaluating the location of all the members in Hyde Park, it became clear that Hyde Park could become a chapter. And shortly after that, that is exactly what happened. During this period, Mildred, a very active member had become the Lake Grove young women's chapter leader.

At that time NSA was having weekly discussion meetings. Most of these meetings were on Saturday afternoon. Since most of the members were young people, it was the norm to have social gatherings after the meetings on Saturday. If there was a party going on, most of the members in the city would find out about it. Usually, the after-parties would be quite a gathering, and that made it possible to meet members from other parts of the city and surrounding areas. It was not unusual to see Mildred and her best buddy, Doris, who was the chapter YWD leader before Mildred. They were very bright and energetic, always together, and impossible not to notice, particularly if you were a young man.

There was a young man in Lake Grove Chapter, who was a YMD District leader (, who told me about his interest in Mildred. Well, I certainly could understand that, and I encouraged him to go for it. However, shortly after that at a social gathering I had an informal dance with Mildred. When I danced with her, there was a strong feeling of familiarity. The truth is I certainly had a type, as far as women were concerned. I guess you could say it was sort of an Angela Davis look that so many young Black women were emulating in those days. I should also mention, that at the time when many black women were overcoming the necessity of having to straighten their hair, the image of the afro was very appealing to me. And Mildred certainly fit the image of the type of women I imagined being with. Sometime later some NSA members went on a camping trip. At one point she and I happened to be in a tent together for a few minutes, just the two of us. We had both just sat down for a few minutes to catch our breath. In that moment I happened to look at her in a different light. Her hair was sort of orange in color from the sunlight, as she set down so free and uninhibited, while we were directly facing one another which was a big turn on to me. At that instant I let out a slight grunt. She said to me, "What's wrong?" I responded," Oh, nothing, I was just thinking of some possibilities." She said no more and neither did I.

Now, in my opinion I was definitely "the marrying type". The problem was, in the past I was not very good at it. So, I had to do what Buddhists call, human revolution. That's where you do some serious changing of oneself. At this point I was thinking about Mildred quite a bit. I remember one time when I was driving, the thought occurred to me that we might end up together. As I have been known to do, I thought to myself," If she and I will end up together, the next car I see will be red. Now, the car that she drove was the little dark blue two-tone Opel. Well, the very next car I saw was a red Opel and it appeared to be the same model that she drove. Although, I might have been jesting somewhat, seeing the red Opel was quite impressive. Around that time Mr. Sasaki, who was the top YMD leader when I begin my practice and later became the top four-divisional (young men, young women, men, and women) leader in Chicago, said to me informally," Bobby, you should think about settling down and getting married." My response was, "Well I do have someone in mind." which was probably a premature statement, but she was on my mind.

Mildred

Around this time, Mildred, Doris, and a friend named Jean, had an apartment together. And of course, I thought that would be a nice place to visit, which I did. I did start getting closer to Mildred. At some point she Invited me to join her at the Travelodge where she swam every day for a workout. And I did just that. However, I couldn't swim although I had wanted to all my life. I started coming every day, the pool was warm, and I loved it. I became determined to learn to swim. While she was swimming,

I was over in the corner trying to teach myself. I felt so confident that I could do it. She would always tell me that I should take swimming lessons, but I would just keep trying over in the corner of the pool. I thought I was making progress, but I could not swim very far.

Then one day I got a set of swim fins and that made all the difference in the world. I could tread water with just the fins alone. At that point I could swim the length of the pool and work on my stroke. I started swimming laps the length of the pool. Then after a while, I took the fins off and tried swimming the width of the pool in the shallow water. Once that worked, I tried the length of the pool. After a while I was able to swim the length of the pool without the fins. In approximately three months I was swimming 50 lengths. That was about 1/2 mile. And then I started doing that every day. That was a big accomplishment in my life. When I was a kid, I had always dreamed of being a proficient swimmer. It really was a dream come true.

We had become an item, and when I went over to meet her parents, I liked them a lot. We had a great meal of her mom's home cooking that reminded me of lot of my own family. Maybe I was a little too relaxed because after the great meal I ended up falling asleep on the couch. Very early in our relationship I did voice my intentions to her, but it seemed to take her about two years to decide to marry me. Of course, that was all good because I just wanted to be with her.

Hyde Park Chapter

After the localization project, it was discovered that there were enough members in the Hyde Park area to become a chapter. So, the chapter was reorganized into five districts. I think it later became one of the two largest chapters in Chicago at that time, at least in terms of attendance and our campaigns. When the chapter began, the leaders were me for Men's Division leader and Shirley Curtwright for Women's Division leader.

It was around this time that I was finally able to stop smoking cigarettes. Mr. Osaki had called a leaders' meeting with the Men's Division Chapter leaders from what I think was a General Chapter, which was a group of at least three Chapters. Mr. Osaki had just had a serious health issue and he was told that he needed to stop smoking cigarettes. The leaders meeting was at my apartment and while we were discussing the dangers of cigarettes, I happened to be smoking one as I was talking about how bad it was. All the guys got a big laugh when somebody brought that to my attention. Maybe to save face, I told Mr. Osaki that if he would stop smoking, I would stop smoking. His reply was, "Would you do that, Bobby?" I said, "I will." So, the next day when I was at the Community Center, Mrs. Osaki tapped me on the shoulder and said, "Mr. Osaki said to tell you he had stopped smoking." That was February 7, 1976. When she said that to me, I had *already* had my last cigarette. My desire to get closer to him was so strong that it was not even difficult. Unlike all the times that I had tried, this was motivated by something much more important to me.

Mr. Osaki

By this time, Mildred and I had been an item for some time and were seriously planning to get married. The coming together of the wedding plan, in and of itself, was very mystical, or at the very least fortunate. Renee, our leader of Lake Grove chapter had also had considerable experience as a caterer and offered to cater the wedding as a wedding gift. A friend of ours in NSA lived in a building which was very beautiful and right on the lakeside. She said that she could get the ballroom for $50, and we could have the reception in that ballroom. One of the young men's members was a rock drummer and offered to bring his band and perform for us as a gift. And David Grilly, who by this time was a very close friend, offered to bring his jazz band. And the Community Center where we would be having the ceremony was free. My friend, Alexander Gbayee, the leader of the Dukorans, who by this time was the Consul General of the Liberia community in Chicago, chauffeured the bride and groom from the ceremony to the reception in his big Lincoln Continental. This all took place on March 25th, 1979.

However, the real ceremony was Friday night the 23rd with the two of us and a very few people. It turned out that the priest who would do the ceremony could only be in town on Friday. The ceremony on Sunday with all the guests was conducted by an NSA leader, Mr. Wright; the same Mr. Wright who had scolded me for my misbehavior with BBJ. And the ballroom reception was incredible. One whole side of the ballroom was glass over-looking Lake Michigan. The photographer was Vandell Cobb, the top photographer for Johnson Publishing, the creator and publisher of such historic magazines like *Ebony* and *Jet*, who just happened to be Mildred's uncle, and the jazz band and the rock bands, who were all friends of ours, were equally as impressive.

The Big Day

Mildred and I we're both leaders in NSA and Mildred had never been to Japan. Later that year in October there was a group of members of NSA going to the head temple in Japan so we decided instead of a honeymoon trip we would hold off for a few months and go to Japan to visit the head temple. Donna, our friend who was the flight attendant, had never been there either and decided to go at the same time, since air travel was free for her, and she wanted to take advantage of that opportunity. Jesse Henderson, the same Jesse who I had assisted in escorting the young women to Hawaii, had flown ahead in advance to help the group of members navigate their way around Japan. although there were a lot of trains and public transportation in getting around Japan, Jesse was incredible in making it all possible for the group of NSA members from Chicago. It was certainly more of a challenge, but it was far better than an ordinary honeymoon. Especially thanks to Jesse.

Knee Surgery

My right knee that I had been having issues with since I was a teenager, was really starting to take its toll on me. I had to get something done. At that time, knee replacement surgery was not as common as it is today, but I decided to check out the possibility. The first doctor I went to told me he would not touch it because it would be infected in about two years because of my rheumatoid arthritis. At that point I was a bit discouraged.

Being a chapter leader of Hyde Park Chapter at that time, I had to attend the five district meetings in the chapter. While attending one of those district meetings, it appeared to me to be a little too intellectual and getting a little boring with a lack of enthusiasm. I began to try to think of ways to encourage them. So, I told them about my knee and the doctor visit that I had just had that left me with little hope. I told them, according to this Buddhist teaching, there is no problem that could not be overcome through faith. So, I told them I am going to show them there is something that I can do about my knee and if not, I will quit practicing this Buddhism. At that, I got an "Aah," that perked everyone up with enthusiasm. I told them I would report back to them at their next meeting. At the very next opportunity I went to another orthopedic physician and inquired about having knee surgery. After examining me he said, "No problem. I can do it." He was a young doctor but told me that he had done replacements that had lasted for ten years. I reported back to the members and got big cheers at the next district meeting, and I let the surgeon do the surgery and the knee lasted for more than 40 years. I think the knee surgery was seven months after the wedding.

Dallas here we come!

Dallas Convention

About three months after my surgery, NSA held a convention in Dallas, TX. Our plan was to have participants from Chicago rent a train to travel to Dallas for the convention. There is a great story about how that came about.

While the members were rehearsing for the performances in Dallas, there was a gentleman with a beard who used to come regularly and enjoyed watching the rehearsals. I don't know if he was an NSA member, but no one seemed to know who he was. So, while they were trying to figure out how they could get this all done with the train scenario, this gentleman overhearing them, said, "Oh, you're trying to charter a train from Chicago to Dallas?" When they said, "Yes," the gentleman pulled out his phone and made a phone call that connected NSA up with the right people to charter the train. It turned out that the older gentleman had some significant connections in the railroad industry. Problem solved. I'm not sure about its validity, but it's a great story.

The NSA members in Chicago were really excited about the convention in Dallas. I think particularly because it was in the middle of winter and Dallas sounded like a great place to be for a convention if you were from Chicago. Mildred and I were no exception. We had every intention of going to that convention. However, at that time Mildred was about five months pregnant. But she was very excited and had no intention of missing it.

Of course, the whole thing was a western theme and everybody from Chicago would be wearing their best western attire. Dallas, TX was a great place to visit in January, particularly if you're living in Chicago, Illinois. The weather was warm, and the trip there on the train with all our NSA Family was a lot of fun. When we got to Dallas with all our western attire, we were cheering and yelling "Yahoo" when we were informed that real Texans don't say "Yahoo," instead, they say "Yee Haw." Lesson learned. The convention was great, with the "East meets West" theme. The opening ceremony was very cool, with Patrick Duffy, famous for his role in the "Dallas" tv show, in his tradition western attire and Toshiro Mifuni, the famous Japanese actor (Torinaga) of Shogun fame, in his traditional eastern attire, rode their horses out to the center of the stadium, to greet and make the point of, "East meets West." Both of whom were a part of our Buddist movement. I was walking around a lot with my walking cane. However, my newly replaced knee was doing so well that I accidentally lost my cane somewhere on the trip. So, I guess you could say I really didn't need it.

Veronica's Entrance

In preparation for the newborn baby, we went through the Lamaze process. I really don't know how much I learned from it all, but I supported Mildred in every way I could. A few months after the convention, May 1st to be exact, Veronica made her entrance. I remember in the doctor's report he said that she had a lusty cry. In my mind, I think that was a hint to her personality. She never hesitates to speak up and is very confident in her own opinion of things. Surprisingly to me, she was always very feminine in her identity. As soon as she was walking and talking, she was adorning herself with ribbons and flowers. I guess I have always thought that sort of thing was pretty much a learned behavior. I really enjoyed the time I spent with her, and she was so young. It was my job to take her to the babysitter, Denise, who was also our friend, in the morning on my way to work. I remember a very loving moment when we were sitting in the car, and she was trying to pretend that she was not looking at me, but when I would catch her eye, she would just laugh. It was sort of like a game we would play.

Of course, we did have some adventures together, too. When we were going to Denise's house one day when it was cold and she was all bundled up in her snow suit, she was running up the stairs and fell and began rolling down the stairs. However, since she always ran ahead of me, I was at the bottom of the stairs to catch her. There was one instance where I was trying to avoid another vehicle on a snowy road and went off the road. In doing so, I hit a concrete post buried under the snow. At that point my car wouldn't start, and I had to call a towing company. We were both okay and the tow truck delivered us to the babysitter. Then, there was the time when we were all at the NSA Community Center and she got stuck behind an upright piano. Fortunately, she was playing with Denise's kids and one of them climbed behind the piano and pulled her out safely.

When I left Rapid Circular Press, I had taken a job as a cameraman at a company called Jay Printing. Ironically the Jays Potato Chip Company in the Chicago area used Jay Printing for most of their printing needs. I don't know how that came about, and I don't think they had any real connection. I liked working at Jay Printing and I liked the personnel there. However, with my new daughter and my health issues, I started developing a strong interest in moving to a warmer climate. There was a pressman at Jay Printing that was always speaking very highly of Arizona. At this point I was getting more determined to move to a warmer climate. I made up a small trifold brochure, that was also a résumé.

On the front panel I had a photograph of me over a light table with a dress tie on, which I never wore at work, and across the top in bold type were the words "Need a good man?" The three panels on the inside were a photo of my family and two panels of my résumé. When the brochure was folded, the back panel had a circular color photograph of a cobblestone wall that was divided into four pieces like a pie. Each section demonstrated a different skill needed by a Graphic Artist. One section was in full color, another section was a duotone, another section was an illustration, and the final section was a grayscale photograph. Each section demonstrated a different technical skill needed for the type of job I was applying for.

Then, around this time I discovered that a young man, Jerry, who had been practicing Buddhism in my chapter when I was a young men's leader, had moved to Arizona. I don't remember how I was able to contact him, but I did, and he invited me to come to Phoenix, Arizona and stay with him to see if I liked it. Liking the idea to visit Jerry in Arizona and checking out the climate there, I decided to visit him. I also mailed a few of my brochure resumés to companies in Phoenix just in case I liked the place. When I got off the plane entering the tunnel over the boarding bridge, it was as if someone had opened an extremely hot oven in my face. That was some impressive heat!

I had always thought of Arizona as being a place of brown dust with tumbleweeds, some cacti and maybe an occasional horse skull here or there. However, when Jerry drove me from the airport to his house, I saw palm trees, grass, lawns, and very clean streets. I was in love with the place almost immediately. When we got to his house I met his wife, Carol, and two sons, Michael, and Jason. Their neighborhood was well kept, as were all the neighborhoods I was able to see during the two weeks I was there.

At some point he took me to visit his friend who had a swimming pool in their yard. She invited me to have a swim in the pool although she had not been in the pool yet that season. In Phoenix, AZ, probably because of the climate, a high percentage of people have pools in their yards, and it is not necessary to be a wealthy person to do so. After reporting back to Mildred, we agreed that I should try to find a job and an apartment in Phoenix. Within the two weeks that I was there I landed a job, secured an apartment, and got my driver's license for Arizona. I guess you could say, I really liked the place.

Within two weeks we had purchased airline tickets for Mildred and Veronica, closed off our business in Chicago, rented a U-Haul and Walter Junior, Mildred's brother, and I packed up all our belongings In the U-Haul, connected my 280Z car to the back of the U-Haul truck, and drove to Arizona to our new apartment in 1 1/2 days. We stopped only for breakfast and gas. When one was driving the other one would rest. I think I picked up Mildred and Veronica at the airport the next day after we got to Phoenix. The whole movement went smoothly, except for one scary moment in Albuquerque when the U-Haul started jackknifing coming down a hill in a rainstorm. I pumped the brakes as best I could and did gain control before anything drastic happened. Although "Pook", the nickname for Mildred's brother, probably wet his pants. Just kidding. He didn't.

Chapter IV
Phoenix, AZ

Our Apartment in Phoenix

The apartment complex, we had just moved into could not have been more than a year old. It had a swimming pool which we both used every day. It was much more convenient than Chicago where we had to go to the Travelodge whenever we wanted to swim which was probably seven miles away from our apartment. Also, this apartment complex was where we first met Julie, our lifelong friend.

Julie and David were a young couple with a daughter, Tarrah, who was slightly younger than our daughter Veronica or Ronnie for short. Mildred and Julie were drawn together with their commonality as young mothers. When Mildred told Julie about our Buddhist practice, she was interested right away. David on the other hand, not so much.

At this point, it was easy for me to get connected to our NSA Organization because Jerry, my friend, was an NSA District Leader. When I came out to visit him, he introduced me to some of the leadership in the Phoenix NSA organization. I also brought with me a letter of recommendation from Frank Nakabayashi, the central figure of the Chicago branch of NSA at the time. When I first got to Phoenix, I participated in the district where Jerry was the men's leader. That district was called, South Phoenix District. His women's counterpart was an excellent and professional vocalist by the name of Sherry Roberson. She was one of the top jazz singers, if not the top jazz singer, in Phoenix at the time. With my being a musician, Sherry and I hit it off right away. I left my position in Chicago as chapter leader of one of the largest NSA chapters in Chicago. We had five districts in the chapter and each district had a district song which they used to liven their meetings. I wrote a district song for South Phoenix District and presented it to Jerry and Sherry. They liked the song a lot and decided to use it at all their district meetings.

At that time, we would have what was called shakubuku campaigns. Shakubuku, is a Japanese word that loosely translates to introducing people to Buddhism. I was told by George J., the headquarters central figure at the time, that from the new excitement and energy South Phoenix District had achieved better results than they had previously. Though I was only in their district for a short time, they continued to use the song for quite some time which made me feel good.

Three months after I arrived in Phoenix two things happened: I landed a job with the second largest lithographic company in Phoenix, Imperial Lithographics (which was my first choice of companies to work for) and, a young NSA district leader resigned his position, and I was able to fill his position immediately because of my experience in Chicago with NSA. The name of the district was, "Capital District."

I decided that the way to kick off a relationship between me and the Capital District members was to call a meeting of everyone who was interested in making the district grow. If I recall correctly, about 10 people showed up and most of them were young. I thought that was a great start. The women's leader of the district was Takako, who was the widow of an American husband and the mother of three, two daughters and a son. It would not be too far-fetched to say that the Japanese women were the backbone of this Buddhist movement in the USA. Many of the first NSA Districts in this country were led by Japanese women and their American spouses.

Capital District had somewhat of a history in the organization in Phoenix. I was told that it was one of the original districts in the Phoenix Chapter of NSA. George J. had also been the leader of Capital District and Phoenix Chapter prior to becoming the leader of the Phoenix Headquarters. I felt privileged to be given the responsibility for that district which was so close to his heart. We had a pretty good run during the time I was the district leader. Usually during shakubuku campaigns, we were in the top two in the headquarters, although usually Number Two because our top competitor was Tempe District, which was in the heart of the

ASU campus area, and they introduced a lot of students. We did as well as we did, in part, because we had the support of Eiko, who was a very powerful young women's leader and the wife of George J. our headquarters leader.

Capital District was in Phoenix Chapter, and the chapter leader was Tim whose wife's name was Betsy and they had a young daughter named Jessica. Tim was the only person I have ever known who married his wife two times, or maybe even three times. I guess that was indicative of their love for each other.

Each chapter was responsible for taking care of the Phoenix NSA Community Center, which had a nice-sized lawn. I don't think there were more than three chapters in Phoenix Headquarters (Although I could be wrong about that). When it was time to cut the grass and prune the bushes, the men from each chapter were supposed to come out and take care of that responsibility. However, during whenever it was our turn to clean up it was always just Tim and myself. It really wasn't a very big job to cut the grass and clean up, but it was a great opportunity to get to know Tim better.

Scott's Entrance

Once we moved to Phoenix, Mildred became pregnant again almost immediately. Of course, whatever else we had going on, the pregnancy became a priority. Just like the first time she was pregnant when I got involved in Lamaze classes, we started preparing for the new birth. Scott made his appearance on April 13th, the following year. Now, we had two kids living in that small apartment. It was paramount that we start finding a bigger place. We really wanted to buy a house, but we never had owned one, and thought that might be an obstacle. We had no real money to put down on a house, but we begin searching anyway.

We began noticing one small house with a swimming pool, but the ad consistently mentioned that they wanted $13,000 in advance. Even though we did not have $13,000, we drove down and looked at the house anyway and loved it. After a while and noticing the house still had not been sold, we decided to reach out again. In talking to the owner, we asked would he be interested in renting the house to us with the option to buy. He told us to come down and look at the house. So, that's exactly what we did. By this time Scott was a little over a year old and a very active kid. When we got to the house, the owner showed us inside. The kids began running around, and we all loved it. My feeling is that the owners just liked the fact that somebody really liked the house as much as we did. So, that very day he gave us the keys to rent it to us. The owner did most of the work trying to get a loan for us. As it turned out by the end of the year 1985, he had secured a loan for us, and we simply had to sign the papers. At this point all we had to do was make the payments. I had a good job and that was not a problem. This whole ordeal turned out to be a major benefit in our lives and I attribute it all to my practice of this Buddhism.

Family Ties in Phoenix

When we first moved to Phoenix, Mildred had a cousin, Gurtha, who already lived there with her husband Tim. Of course, we connected with them right away. Gurtha eventually moved her mother, Aunt Susanna, to Phoenix. The first two years we were living in Phoenix, Mildred was a stay-at-home mom. However, when it was time for Mildred to go back to work, Aunt Suzanna volunteered to babysit for us. Mildred was an editor by trade, and it seemed to be quite easy for her to land a job. At one point the firm that she was working for enabled her to set up an office in our home. To spend the maximum time with our kids, she would find creative ways to work from home, sometimes doing freelance editing for authors.

When going into her office was unavoidable, we always had Aunt Suzanna who was a colorful person with a good sense of humor. Much of the time she could be heard singing those old

Black southern spirituals from her childhood in Georgia. She was very funny, and the kids liked her a lot, so it all worked out very well.

Imperial Lithographics

When I first visited Phoenix two weeks before we moved out there, I got a job with a small company called Progressive Litho. Three months after I moved to Phoenix, I got a job with Imperial Lithographics. At that time that was my first choice of all the companies that I had seen in Phoenix. My first position there was in a department called contacting. After I proved myself in that department, they moved me up to another department called 4-color stripping.

After being successful in that department, the management brought in some new equipment, a large computer which created different types of masks to burn images on plates for a printing press. The equipment was made by a company called Gerber. I was chosen to be the one of two people to operate the Gerber. With my supervisor and Vicki, the other person, we flew out to Los Angeles to be trained for the Gerber Auto Prep. As it turned out when we returned to Phoenix, I was the main one that was interested in running that department which consisted of three rooms, one room for the operator and computer, another room for the plotter and another room for the final film to be processed, cut, and made ready to make plates.

It was at that time that Apple was beginning to become a major force in the graphics community. At the encouragement of Kevin, who later became Vicki's husband, I took a computer course for Macintosh computers. In addition to that I took some courses in graphics software like Quark Express and then later in some Adobe products that would soon lead the way in the graphics community. That was the beginning of my computer graphics world and I never looked back.

As it turned out, I worked at Imperial for 13 years which was the longest I had ever been on any job. I also made some lifetime friends there like Vicki and D.J. I got closer to Vicki when we were both in L.A. to learn about the Gerber Auto Prep. D.J. aka Denis and I put in valuable bonding time getting high in the dark room. DJ was an ex-marine and I just found out recently that he had passed away. All our servicemen are my heroes, but I really appreciated the time I was able to spend with him. All the time I worked with him he didn't know I played the saxophone. The first time he attended one of my gigs he came on stage at the break and gave me a big kiss and said, "I had no idea." Rest in peace, Buddy!

One thing that happened during the early years that I worked for Imperial, was that I had wrist surgery on my right hand. Although my rheumatoid arthritis was mostly under control, it was still active. My right wrist was fusing and turning to the side. Somehow, I was connected to a hand surgeon who offered to straighten my hand and put in a hinge that would allow me to bend my wrist. After discussing the matter with the doctor, we decided to do local anesthesia. I asked him if I could I watch the surgery and he agreed. That was a very surreal experience! Watching them cut open my wrist and cut into my bone while seeing my hand flopped over mostly unattached brought on a feeling I can't adequately describe. But, believe me, it was bizarre. The results of the surgery were good, and I was very pleased. Later there would be another surgery to tweak some minor issues but he would not allow me to watch that one. I think someone must have advised him against it.

Phoenix Chapter

Tim and Betsy decided they were going to move to another city, leaving Phoenix. When they left, I became the men's chapter leader of Phoenix Chapter. I'm not sure when, but the organization stopped putting emphasis on the central figure and more on divisional leadership (Men's, women's, Young Men's, and Young Women's), working as a team. I was very proud to be the men's chapter leader of NSA in a relatively short period of time. To me, it was a special gift from the universe. It was like, "Welcome home, Bobby, this is where your mission lies."

There was one district leader in the chapter, Gillon, who was also part of the LGBT community, and he was struggling with HIV. Once when I was visiting him, he was lying there lifeless, hardly able to breathe. He had this sound in his throat that sounded like what we used to call the death rattle. Everyone was chanting hard for him. I was so convinced he wasn't going to make it that I was chanting he would have a smooth transition. As it turned out, he got through that night, then another night and then after a while he was back on his feet and doing regular activities. I was extremely impressed with Gillon. He lived actively for another two years. However, in the end that demon would claim his life, but it never took away his spirit to fight.

Mr. (Ted) Osaki

Not so long after I moved to Phoenix, my absolute favorite leader from Chicago purchased a home in Phoenix and moved here. It is my guess that he was encouraged to do so because of his health issues. But, for whatever reason I certainly thought it was my benefit. He had already left Chicago before I did, and I think he was a leader in California for a while. But, in any case he moved here, and I was glad. I remember one day when I was in the lobby of the Community Center, I heard someone describing a task for the young men's division leader at the time. And I overheard Mr. Osaki say to them," Let Bobby do it, he will get it done." That was absolutely music to my ears, to know that he had such trust in me.

While talking to him at one point he did let me know that he had started smoking again. However, because of our relationship I was able to stop smoking, something I had never been able to do before. There was no way that I was ever going to start back again, and I thanked him for that. He did pass away maybe a year or so after that and each chapter chief led a *toso* (chanting session) for one hour at his home for his smooth transition. I was extremely proud to be able to lead the chanting for the first hour.

My Last Tozan (Pilgrimage)

Around the middle to late 80s I had an opportunity to go to Japan which would be my third time. When Nichiren was exiled to Sado Island where he had written two of his major Gosho (writings), The Opening of the Eyes and The Object of Devotion for Observing One's Mind, his followers would risk their lives to go visit him and bring him food, etc. With that same spirit it had become a tradition to make a pilgrimage to the head temple. Somewhere in the middle to late 80s I had the opportunity to make that trip. At that time, I only remember two people from Phoenix who made that trip. That was me and a young woman by the name of Mary Anne. The activities were mostly ceremonial events like the airing of old Gohonzon scrolls and other paper documents. Since we were both from the same area, we were given lockers next to each other to store our personal belongings while we were attending activities on the temple grounds. The lockers were so close to one another that one day when we were both going into our lockers at the same time, we literally bumped heads and I must say it was quite a solid bump. I remember thinking, "Wow, what kind of karma must we have to deserve that?" I never figured that out, but we did get a chance to chant to the Dai Gohonzon, (a Gohonzon originally inscribed by Nichiren "for all mankind") and as it turned out that would be my last chance I would have to do so, and a little 'bump on the head' would not change that. We did have a lot of fun with some Japanese phrases that sounded like English phrases. One phase, in particular, that they kept saying over and over to us was something that sounded like, "Give *me some of that stuff.*" And if I'm not mistaken, they would usually bow when they would say it. All in all, I was grateful to have been able to make that pilgrimage particularly since it would be my last opportunity.

April 11, 1991

April 11th, 1974, was the date I received my Omamori Gohonzon a miniature Gohonzon which can be worn on the person or placed in a portable altar when traveling. I was very proud to get an Omamori Gohonzon and immediately went out and had that date engraved on the back of the silver case which housed the Omamori. In 1991 April 11th I had the most serious car accident that I had ever had in my life.

In Phoenix they had a street (7th Street) which had a reversible lane right in the center of it. In the mornings that lane would be southbound, heading toward the downtown area. After 4:00 PM that same lane would become northbound, heading away from the downtown area. Of course, the whole idea was to facilitate the direction in which most of the traffic was heading. They had a similar program in Chicago where they use reversible lanes in the same manner.

On that day, I was heading southbound on 7th Street, heading toward the downtown area in the reversible lane when suddenly a taxicab entered the reversable lane not realizing that I was in his blind spot. The cab hit my car and forced me into oncoming traffic. I had a head-on collision with a Nissan Pathfinder. I was dazed and confused but I heard people's voices. I heard one man say, "It was my fault. I was changing lanes." I looked around to see if I was OK when I noticed a bone sticking out of my thigh. There was a woman that used to ride with me in the mornings to work. Fortunately for her, she did not make it that day because the passenger side was pretty much demolished. She would not have made it alive. I do remember them putting me on a stretcher and rushing me to the hospital. After that, things got a little fuzzy, but when I did wake up in the hospital, D.J. from my job was standing next to the bed. Sometime after that my primary care physician came in, Dr. Nafisi. I didn't realize he was my primary care physician but the fact that he was there made a big impression on me, and he is still my primary care physician today, more than 30 years later.

Of course, when they got me to the hospital, they did emergency surgery on, putting back together all 12 pieces of my femur with a supporting rod and 12 screws to hold it all together. The surgeon said to me he was 80% certain that I would not lose my leg. It should be noted that this all happened to the femur on my right leg which was the same leg of my knee replacement from 1979.

X-ray frrom accident.

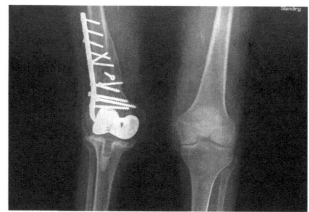

When I got back to work my supervisor, Debbie, told me that the owner and president of the company asked her what she had planned to do about me and my situation. She told him she would do nothing if I could continue to do the work. After I got out of the hospital, I was on crutches for six months, but I came to work every day.

It was only when I was looking over my insurance claims that I realized the date of the accident was the same date engraved on the back of my Omamori Gohonzon case. Moving forward, one day shy of 30 years from that date (April 10th 2021) I ran a stop sign and a woman ran into me. When I called my insurance company and told them that it was my fault, they said no problem that they would take care of it and the fees that I would normally have to pay were waived because of my good driving record (smile). I am not sure how to evaluate all of that, but I don't really believe much in coincidences.

Stories in Veronica's and Scott's early development

When we first moved into the apartment in Phoenix, one of our neighbor's had a girl about the same age as Veronica. At that age Veronica was not shy and exuded confidence for a three-year-old. One simple way we would do Veronica's hair was to put it in two ponytails which was kind of fluffy and bushy. Her friend wanting to be like Veronica, which was not really going to happen because she was white with straight hair. She would still pressure her mom to fix her hair like Veronica's. Her mom would try to accommodate her, sort of.

After we moved into our house and Veronica started to attend school, most of her classmates were white, and during her young life her hair became a non-issue. She has grown up to be a confident woman, an X-ray technician, and a mother of four.

Scott's stories are a much scarier. One day while I was hanging out in the pool with Scott. I was on one of those floating mattresses and he was all over the pool with his water wings, I happened to look up and he must have jumped off the diving board with his arms up, because his wings were floating by themselves and he was struggling, trying to get his head above the water in the deep end of the pool. When I saw that I immediately dived in the pool, swam to him, got him to the ladder and put him on the pool deck. He staggered away from a lack of oxygen. It was the scariest thing I have ever experienced with either of my kids.

When Scott was a teenager, he got a job and bought an old Cadillac which I think was popular with the kids he hung out with, at age 16. One night when he was on his way home while waiting at a red stoplight, someone drove up next to him and started spraying bullets from the back to the front of his car. The one bullet that would have hit him got lodged into the metal work of the door. Life is clearly the most valuable thing we have, yet very fragile. I am sure those experiences have at least given him some understanding of that. He must also feel that something or someone is looking out for him. Today Scott is living in Mexico as a successful businessman.

From NSA to SGI

"In November 1991, the Nichiren Shoshu priesthood, under the leadership of its high priest, Nikken Abe, excommunicated all of more than 10 million SGI members. His hope was to pull a large percentage of Soka Gakkai members into Nichiren Shoshu temples. That didn't happen." This is an excerpt from the SGI website addressing our "Spiritual Independence." (Please visit the sgi-usa.org website for more information on the "Spiritual Independence.")

Soka Gakkai (Value Creation Society) was founded by two Japanese educators, Tsunesaburo Makiguchi and his fellow schoolteacher and young disciple, Josei Toda, in 1930 Japan. Originally it was called Soka Kyoiku Gakkai which meant Value Creation Education Society, but later the word Education (Kyoiku) was dropped. I found it very interesting that some of today's modern thinking of how life created itself was based on life's fundamental drive to create value. Makiguchi felt that the teachings of Nichiren Buddhism were most in line with his way of thinking and therefore encouraged all its members to practice Nichiren Buddhism. So, they all joined Nichiren Shoshu.

Between the years of 1937 and 1945 Japan was at war and trying to get all the Japanese people to rally around the Shinto religion to unify Japan during the war. However, both Makiguchi and Toda, his disciple, refused to give up their practice of Nichiren Buddhism, and because they didn't comply, they were both imprisoned. Makiguchi, at 76 died in prison and Toda was released July 3rd, 1945, six weeks before Japan surrendered which was after the atomic bomb had been dropped.

At that time Nichiren Shoshu was a few thousand people, but by the time I joined in 1971 they had millions of members, most of whom were from the Soka Gakkai. NSA Nichiren Shoshu of America and all the lay believers of Nichiren Shoshu was led by Daisaku Ikeda, (a responsibility given to him by the 66th High Priest Nittatsu Shonin) and he (Daisaku Ikeda) gave Nichiren Shoshu priesthood the highest respect and supported them. After some time of that support, the priesthood appeared to become arrogant and started expressing an air of superiority to the lay believers.

The concept of superior and inferior human beings is something I have fought against all my life as a young Black man growing up in Knoxville in the southern United States. It was an idea contrary to Nichiren's teachings where he wrote: *"Shakyamuni Buddha who attained enlightenment countless kalpas ago, the Lotus Sutra that leads all people to Buddhahood, and we ordinary human beings are in no way different or separate from one another. To chant Myoho-renge-kyo with this realization is to*

153

inherit the ultimate Law of life and death. This is a matter of the utmost importance. " (The Heritage of the Ultimate Law of Life)

Shakyamuni taught the equality of all living beings at a time when the caste system of India strictly separated and confined people, and women were seen as inferior to men. He left his life as a prince of the Shakya clan to live among the common people to learn the meaning of life, and to discover how to eliminate the sufferings of birth, aging, sickness, and death from all humanity.

In my opinion, other than Nichiren himself, there is no other human being more responsible for spreading Nichiren Buddhism around the world to lay believers than Daisaku Ikeda. I say that without hesitation. He literally got on a plane and flew around the world setting up small districts with leaders that sometimes had no experience at all with Buddhism. And most importantly, it worked. These lay believers respected and followed him, and so do I. After the 66th High Priest Nittatsu passed away, things took a turn for the worse.

Nikken Abe became the High Priest in a seriously questionable manner. At that point Nikken Abe started demonstrating what appeared to be an extreme jealousy about all the attention and respect we were giving to Daisaku Ikeda. The excommunication of all the SGI members was a desperate move to change that scenario. Of course, at that point SGI members just rallied around Daisaku Ikeda. It seemed to me that Nikken became so consumed with anger and jealousy that he just started *blowing shit up.* By 1998 he had destroyed the grand main temple, the Sho Hondo and SGI would go on to become what is considered by most the largest Buddhist and peace movement in the world. I would call us, The True Bodhisattvas of the Earth.

In the "Emerging from the Earth," chapter (fifteenth) of the 28 chapters of the Lotus Sutra, the first of the sutra's essential teachings (latter fourteen chapters), Shakyamuni introduces the four leaders of the Bodhisattvas of the Earth. Those leaders were

154

Superior Practices, Boundless Practices, Pure Practices and Firmly Established Practices. I think I can safely say that believers in Nichiren Buddhism, including Nichiren himself, believe that the scenario as it is described in the Lotus Sutra is a real prediction of how this Buddhism will spread, and that he, Nichiren, is "Superior Practices, who is the leader of the Bodhisattvas. Because of the tremendous results SGI has already achieved worldwide, I think we of the SGI are the predicted Bodhisattvas of the Earth. At one time I would have been very skeptical of any claim of predicting future events, but after experiencing the scene of seeing Sucker, my pet cat, lying dead in a detailed dream three days before it occurred removed all doubt, I might have had about the possibility of seeing the future.

When Nikken Abe excommunicated all the SGI, he was helping us fulfill our purpose. I would like to think he was aware of that.

R. A. Raises its Ugly Head

During the time that I worked at Imperial I started having pain in my right hip. When I would bend it, it was not smooth and very painful. When I went to see a doctor, as I suspected my hip was deteriorating. The solution was hip replacement. Not very long after I recovered from the surgery, I began to have pain in my left hip, which in fact did lead to another hip replacement.

I now had both hips and one shoulder replaced so it was obvious that the R. A. had not finished with me. It didn't happen all at once and I really didn't lose much time off work other than sick leave and vacation time, but it was still proving to be a major obstacle. However, one should know that your hip could slip out of joint if you aren't careful. When my first grandson, Hashim was a toddler, I twisted my body to reach down and pick him up quickly, however I soon discovered that was a bad idea. I had most of my weight on my right leg and I threw out my right hip which meant I had to go to the hospital and have it reset. I had a similar incident at a convenience store when I turned quickly to pick up something off the floor and I threw my left hip out. It was more of a hassle because I was in a public place. I learned to be more cautious when I'm turning and picking up stuff.

Replacing my right shoulder was a bigger obstacle for me, because it meant I could no longer swim laps in the pool, at least not with the traditional forward crawl stroke. I have heard that they have developed new shoulder replacements with full extension of the joint. That is certainly not enough to encourage me to get another surgery at my age. Besides, since then I had the left shoulder replaced and living with little or no pain in either shoulder works for me. I just find other ways of doing my cardiovascular exercise.

Gongyo and Daimoku

You may be thinking that I talk about losing joints like knees and shoulders as if it's no big deal, but that's not the case. Each time I would lose a joint, it was initially devastating. The first joint, my right knee, was the most devastating. When it got to the point that moving the joint was terribly painful, I knew it was going to have to be replaced. If you recall our daily practice in SGI Buddhism is doing gongyo, which is the reciting of a portion of the Lotus sutra and then daimoku, chanting, Nam-myoho-renge-kyo (It usually takes me about 3 1/2 minutes to recite the sutra portion and then one can chant daimoku as much or as long as they like.

Chanting the words Nam-myoho-renge-kyo is called daimoku which literally means prayer. I will explain that more deeply later. Reciting it once is one daimoku Chanting daimoku is, for me, the ultimate form of meditation because the phrase itself describes what you are doing and what you are chanting to, which is the entity of your own life as well as the life of the universe and I do it every day, morning, and evening, and have been consistent since February of 1972. Just imagine a football team before a game pumping themselves up with a chant to increase their determination and unity. To me, it's a little bit like that, but on a much more profound level. At that time, I was chanting at least one hour a day. I was changing all the lemons into lemonade, or, as the Buddhists would call it, "Changing poison into medicine." With all that chanting, no joint replacement or anything else was going to bring me down. And by the way, you don't need to chant loud to chant with determination.

Leaving Imperial

During the time that I was at imperial, a lot happened. The owner and founder of the company had passed away and his son-in-law had taken on the responsibility of running the company. A smaller printing company had shut down and Imperial merged with at least part of that company. At that time, we knew someone was going to get laid off, but I was too arrogant to think that it could possibly be me. However, in looking back, I had been told that I was the third highest paid person in the department, and I knew one of the new guys could run the Gerber Auto Prep, so looking back, it was probably a no-brainer business decision.

The person who got laid off was me. I had worked at Imperial Lithographics, the company where I most enjoyed working for **13** years. This may be a good time to address my relationship with the number **13**. I was born at **1308** Dora St in Knoxville. From there we moved to **1333** Western Avenue in Knoxville. My only brother was born on the **13**th of July. I began my Buddhist practice on Friday, August the **13**th in 1971. My son was born on April **13**th, which was **13** years from the time I began my Buddhist practice, and my first grandson was born on the **13**th of September. There is more as you will see as I unfold my life to you. So, although I didn't know it at the time, after **13** years it was time for me to leave Imperial in 1996.

Between 1996 and 2004 I had 5 jobs. I don't remember a lot about any of them, but they paid the bills. In 2004 I went to work for Techniprint of Arizona. However, during that time I was more active with my music.

Reviving my musical activity

At some point before 1996, our local SGI organization had moved into a new community center which was closer to the downtown area of Phoenix and was in a business area. It was a large office building which SGI had purchased for a good price, but many of the SGI members thought it was too large for us. It was a three-story building and the whole time we were there we never used more than the first two floors.

Once I joined NSA in 1971 most of my music activity was a part of NSA activities except for a little work that I was getting with the Dukorans. In NSA we seemed to always be preparing for some activity that entailed my practicing in the band. Although at one point I was put in charge of the drum section and played a marching snare, I spent a longer time heading up the saxophone section and playing alto saxophone. My playing improved a lot during that experience. When I got to Phoenix, one of the first meetings I attended at the community center (if not the first), I played piano chords behind some skit that was part of the meeting. That was my first performance of many of the SGI meetings in Phoenix.

I am not sure about the exact timeline, but it seems likely that leaving my job at Imperial was a good motivation for me to start focusing on my music again. George Nakamura, who is currently the Southwest Zone leader of SGI, and a graduate of Soka University in Japan has been the top leader in this area for almost as long as I can remember, granted me a key to the new community center on 7th Street to allow me to practice my saxophone. I went there during the day and practiced, as a musician might call it "woodshedding." I certainly got proficient with my saxophone. For a short time, I was playing with a light rock band where I was told that I was playing my horn a little too much, which I corrected right away. We then had an audition for a job we did not get but the people who were hiring us said, they did however like the saxophone. That was the last time I played with that band.

At one point I was at one of Sherry Roberson's gigs, and liked her saxophone player, Ted Beladin. I thought he was very good, and after approaching him, I started taking lessons from him. At his encouragement I also started going to jam sessions which in many cases were really Blues jam sessions. The idea was to get to know musicians in the Phoenix area. At one jam session I ran into Mike Halperin, a keyboard player who I had met in SGI. I had heard that he played piano, but I had never heard him play. After getting together at his place a few times we decided to add a drummer and consider getting some work. There was a fellow member in SGI, George Meade, who played drums. The three of us got a few gigs and played at several SGI activities and were beginning to gel as a trio. After a while George and his wife decided to move to Indiana so we had to replace him with another drummer named John who was an excellent drummer. (John, wherever you are my apologies for not remembering your last name).

I will say that over the years my most rewarding musical experiences were with NSA/SGI. For one thing I noticed there wasn't as much friction of egos with the Buddhist bands as there was with the other bands that I've played in. We also had large productions with dance groups, choirs, etc. We would have conventions with musical and dance groups from different cities that were mostly performed by youth. We would rehearse our groups until they got quite professional in appearance.

There was one performance, in particular, that comes to mind. SGI was giving a performance on the campus of the University of Arizona. Among the performances was a band from Phoenix and a band from Denver. Our band had been working with a young man, Dustin Morrissey, who had never worked with our band before, but he sounded a lot like the lead singer in Santana's "Smooth." When we got to auditorium with our equipment, a young man ran up to us and said, "Would you guys' mind going on first?" I got the distinct impression that the band from Denver did not want to look like an opening band. Without hesitation we said, "No, we don't mind at all." So, we opened with "Smooth." The young people in the audience were literally dancing in the aisles. It was a great opening number. We then followed up with," Picking up the Pieces," by the "Average White Band, and then "Brick House," by The Commodores. To put it frankly, we killed it. In that case being the first band out of the gate was, exactly, where you would want to be.

AZ Performers Inc.

After realizing that I knew quite a few musicians and other artists like clowns, some from SGI and others that I knew from jam sessions, I decided to form a booking agency. In a very short time, I collected the consent and necessary information from the artists, made up some business cards and a website and got a couple of gigs for the artists and then incorporated. There was a lot of entertainment in the Phoenix area but, as I found out, most of the venues that I was exploring were already taken by C C Jones Musical Productions. It was a lot of fun, but hard work. After about a year I decided to throw in the towel. After all, I always seemed to be able to get a graphics job. It was about this time that I would land my last job in graphics.

Minister of Ceremonies

One day, probably in the '90s, after we had split from the Nichiren Shoshu priesthood), a fellow leader, Dean Morrisey was talking to another leader, George Nakamura, about something that seemed to me sort of uncomfortable. As I was passing by the two of them, Dean turned to me and asked me if I would like to be the person who would officiate weddings. And, with very little thought, I said, "Sure." George seemed to be okay with it,

160

so that's how I was selected to be a Minister of Ceremonies. After filling out a few forms that registered me with the State of Arizona, I was the official Minister of Ceremonies in the local area of SGI. The very first ceremony I officiated was for George's brother, Hiroshi Nakamura. I was extremely nervous, but after that first one they began to be sort of fun. I held that position for what I think was about 3 maybe 4 years. I enjoyed the weddings, but the memorial ceremonies were much more profound. There were times when I would literally have a strong sense of the deceased. Eric Hardy's memorial was one that sticks out the most to me. He was a young African American who was gay with quite feminine mannerisms. To me he seemed sharp and alert. One day another young man jokingly got in front of Eric with his fist up in an offensive boxing position. Eric immediately brought both fists up into a defensive stance and said," Oh, okay. Let's see what you've got!" The other guy laughed and walked away. I was particularly impressed with how comfortable Eric was in that scenario. I don't know his health history, but he seemed to have suddenly gotten sick and passed away. It turned out he had been a U. S. Marine with medals and honors. His ceremony began with a military ceremony. At the end of the ceremony, I was scheduled to give closing words. With all the things that people were saying it seemed that they were all purposely avoiding the fact that he was outgoingly gay. When I got up to give closing words, I pointed that out, and in doing so everyone chuckled a sigh of relief. I stressed that he was an honorable Buddhist, an honorable Marine and an honorable human being and being gay would not lessen his honor in any way. It was clear to me that he had reached a level of honor that any man would be proud to claim.

Eric Hardy

One of the most significant changes in my perspective of the man/woman relationship came from a passage I use to read in the wedding address. *"A man is like the wings of a bird, a woman like the body. If the wings and the body become separated, then how can the bird fly?"* (Letter written to Lay Nun Sennichi, the wife of Abutsubo, WND 1 pg. 1043, in1280). Of course, this metaphor was used to emphasize the unity between husband and wife. However, since being a minister of ceremonies, and reading this passage many times, I have come to look at the mom or woman as the center of the family unit and the man or father as more of a supporting and protecting roll. Of course, this is a definite parting with traditional patriarchy which I think was/is prevalent in most cultures for many years. Which, I suspect, is a scenario that came about through not much more than brute dominance in the early, primitive, development of humanity.

Techniprint/AZ

One of those five jobs I had after leaving Imperial was at a place called Drum Printing where I worked with a young woman by the name of Kari, who was their graphics artist. I don't remember the exact circumstances, but she left Drum Printing and the next time I heard from her, she called me and told me the company she was working for was looking for a graphic artist and asked me if I would be interested. I told her "Yes" and she gave me the address to Techniprint where she was working. When I got to Techniprint, they gave me some text and a photo or graphic and asked me to design a flyer or maybe an ad. I did it, they liked it, and they hired me. It was pretty much just like that. The owner of Techniprint, and I think the founder, was Dick Smith. I only remember seeing him daily for the first couple of years. After that, it seems that he and his wife Charlotte, were there less frequently. At that point it seems that two of the senior management employees, Rick and Daleena were running the company. It was about this time that my trio was opening at a restaurant called Little Mamas. I had invited the employees to the show and a few of them came down to check it out, that included Art and his son, Steven, about 7 or 8 years old. After a while Art informed me that his son, Steven, wanted to play saxophone. I'm sure he asked me for some advice, and I gave him the best advice I could. Steven ended up getting an alto saxophone, which was a good student Yamaha model. Over the years, Art informed me that Steven was taking saxophone lessons and was practicing regularly.

An Awakening

Around this time, I had what I consider an awakening experience in my life. I was pondering the guidance that I have heard many times concerning one's heavy karma. Of course, since I was a child with rheumatoid arthritis, I would say that was the main motivation for trying to find a power beyond what I knew existed in my young age. Being brought up in a Christian environment, I prayed many times to change my situation, but nothing I recognized came about. After beginning my practice of this Buddhism more than 50 years ago I have been thoroughly convinced that this was the power I had been looking for. The guidance that I was referring to, was the idea that sometimes we may choose a very difficult life to prove the validity of this practice. I have chanted hours a day for many years.

One day, at a weak moment while I was chanting, the thought came to my mind, "Why the fuck would I have chosen this karma?" Although the thought was very strong, I continued to chant without hesitation. Sometime later I was having an incredible day, full of confidence and appreciation for the ability to control my life. I was feeling very empowered by the practice of Buddhism when suddenly like a little panic attack the thought occurred to me, "How can I be sure that experiencing this practice is not just a one-time thing? "As I thought, the reality is I may never experience this teaching again in my eternal existence no matter what I think about it now. At that moment, like a little voice in my head, I heard these words, "That's why you would choose this life with your heavy karma." I understood immediately and I was elated at the words of that little voice in my head. It made so much sense and a major change in the way I look at my health karma. I treasure my karma and most of all I treasure this practice it has led me to.

Princess Tarrah Jewel

One day in 2006 I received a phone call from hell. Julie, who was the very first friend we had when we moved to Phoenix with a daughter a year younger than Veronica, our daughter, was on the other end of the call. She was obviously distraught when she said to me, "Tarrah overdosed last night and died." That's a message that you never want to hear from a loved one. I think of all the drugs that I did in my young life. I've done almost every kind of street drug you can imagine, even stuff I couldn't identify. That could very easily have been me. As a young man I never was particularly cautious. About twice in my life, I overdosed to the point that it took me about four days to return to reality. At least in one case I was so far gone I could only remember the word "Bobby," but I wasn't sure what it meant. Having said all that, what was the difference? In all the few times I saw her after she had grown up, she always seemed to have it together. She was beautiful, poised, and graceful and I always assumed she would have a successful life. So, imagine how my heart dropped when I heard those words.

As it turned out I would be in Florida at a conference at the time of the memorial service, but Mildred would be there to show our support. To show my support, I got as many photos of Tarrah as possible from Julie and took my favorite recording of my quartet at the time and made a video presentation of Tarrah for the memorial service. Right after the memorial service, while I was still at the conference, I talked to Mildred, and she said the memorial service was incredible. There were more than 400 people in attendance, which I am pretty sure was more people than I had ever seen in the Phoenix Buddhist Center, and it was very moving, and everything went off perfectly.

A few years later while I was on front desk duty at the Buddhist Center, a couple of people were remembering it all. I then shared the original phone call. As I described it, I relived it. But this time I could not hold back my tears. That was surprising to me.

Red and Dad

Red and Dad are Mildred's parents. Red, whose name was Amanda, was given the name "Red" by Mildred's dad, Walter, or "Goober", as Red called him, because of her hair color when she was young. I called Mildred's dad, Dad simply because Mildred called him Dad, although there may have been some underlying feelings since I was 6 years old when my father passed, and I never experienced having a father beyond that age. When we moved to Phoenix and after Scott was born, Red and Dad came to visit us when we were still living at the apartment and then also after we had moved into our house. When the kids got a little older, they had the opportunity to go spend some time with their grandparents in Evanston IL which they thoroughly enjoyed.

Mildred's brother, Walter Jr. or as everyone called him, Pook, was usually on the road working for the NBA as an Assistant Coach or Scout. Red and Dad were usually in this big two-story house plus a basement by themselves. A few years into the 21st Century I started hearing from Mildred about Dad struggling with his health. By the year 2012 his health had taken a toll on him, and he passed away. Red, who had already fallen and injured herself, was not able to take care of herself and the consensus was that she should come to Arizona and stay with us since we had an extra bedroom and Mildred would be able to care for her. Since everyone agreed, that's exactly what happened.

The Last Year at Techniprint

All in all, Techniprint was a pretty nice place to finish up my graphics career. It had a bit of a family atmosphere and sometimes on Fridays we would grill bratwurst in the parking lot and drink beer. And then there was Tim, the bindery guru, who also played guitar and who joined me at a few jam sessions in a couple of Blues bars around town, and a couple of studio-recording sessions. Today, we still touch base during the AZ Cardinals football season.

2016 was my last year at Techniprint and I was 72 years young, and management was already starting to ask questions like, "Bobby when were you thinking about retiring?" I had already started collecting Social Security income about five years prior to that and had bought a new silver color Genesis Coupe, which was my favorite car, and feeling pretty good about everything. It was about this time that I was having a strong desire to introduce someone from Techniprint to my Buddhist ideology. You see, to me, Buddhism explains religion with all its infinite power in a way that completely corresponds with all we know to be scientifically factual. So, sometimes I have a strong desire to just tell someone about it. Which is, in reality, a part of the process of making the whole world peaceful and happy.

So, in my mind I was looking for someone young and intelligent. In the whole company the person who popped in my mind was Pete Knopp. Pete hadn't been there very long, but he looked the part to me. Glenn, one of the long-time employees was retiring, so, the Friday of his last week would be his retirement party. The party went very smoothly, and everyone was enjoying themselves. At some point Pete came over to say a few encouraging words to Glenn.

I had heard that Pete's girlfriend was having some health issues, so I asked him how she was doing. He responded and we struct up a conversation. In a short time, I was pouring my Buddhist heart out, mostly by describing my concept of the infinite nature of the universe in its microcosm and macrocosm. He told me later that was the concept that made the greatest impression on him. At that time, I shared with him the strange connection I had with number **13** and after a while I happened to ask when his birthday was, and he said February **13**. At first, I thought he was pulling my leg, but as it turned out he was not. At the time, although I didn't realize it, the Friday of the party where all this took place was May **13**. I think this kind of thing in the spiritual community is called *synchronicity*, which also applies to instances of seeing future events, like my dream of Sucker's death. Or in some religious communities it might be called little miracles. Pete did join SGI and on his entrance exam, which was optional, he did surprisingly well. I feel we have a very special connection in the world of spirituality, and I am optimistic about where it's going.

In the end at Techniprint I don't remember the details, but I am sure they had at least begun hinting on my retirement, so I retired. I will always feel like a part of their family. I finished my stay there at the end of December 2016, which was I think, two months shy of my **13**th year.

Whiskers & Oni

The first dog I had was "Dusty," a little boxer mix. I got him at a time when my grandmother never allowed dogs in the house, but for some reason she took a liking to Dusty. He never got to be an adult dog because he got out of the yard and was hit by a car. My next dog was "Skippy." Skippy got out of the yard and was also hit by a car. The next dog I had was Ghanja and shortly after that I got Sucker, both while I was still married to Gina.

Whiskers

In 1986 when Veronica was five years old, one of Mildred's co-workers' cat had kittens and she offered one of the kittens to Mildred, and she accepted. At some point they saw a sign with the word "Whiskers" on it and that's how she got her name. What we didn't realize was that this area, Palo Verde Hills, is somewhat of a mountainous area, and has a healthy coyote population. When we first moved into our house, all the windows had wrought iron bars on them. There would be many nights when something would chase Whiskers up between the bars and she would fight them off through the bars.

Veronica at that age was terribly afraid of dogs and quite allergic to cats. However, she really liked Whiskers, who also helped Veronica overcome her fear of animals. There were times when she would be petting Whisker while sniffling with a runny nose. However, in a fairly short time she overcame her allergies from cats. Whiskers was obviously good for Veronica. Whiskers would live to be 19 years old, and Veronica was 24 when Whiskers died. We no longer have the bars over the windows, so that's one reason we will probably never have another cat while living here in this neigborhood.

In November 2011 I happened to be at my doctor's office,

and I was parked across the street in the parking lot of a veterinarian hospital. As I was walking toward my car, I walked past a young man with his trunk open and there was a litter of Siberian Husky pups in it. When I investigated the trunk of his car all the memories of Ghanja came back to me. So, I got the phone number from the young man that was driving the car. When I got home, I presented the idea of having a dog to Mildred. After some discussion she reluctantly agreed. So, I contacted the young man and arranged to purchase one of the puppies. Of course, it was a female like Ghanja with the same colorings of gray that she had. So, this is the thing. I have believed in reincarnation for some time. So, allow me to explain why.

Ever since I was a kid, I was fascinated with hypnosis, which seemed to be quite accurate with details when regressing to pass events that you may have forgotten. Time after time one could regress all the way back to a past life. However, many in the scientific community would explain that by saying when the mind under hypnosis would come to a deadlock it would simply start creating stuff (or making shit up) I always thought that was a shaky explanation and although there may be some truth to that, I think they were mainly eliminating the possibility of reincarnation. I never had much confidence in that explanation.

Then there was the time when I had telephone duty on Christmas day at the Chicago NSA community center. A holiday was the worst time to be on phone duty because there was nobody there and it was very boring. So, I chanted that something would happen, and I would be very glad to have done phone duty that day. So, while sitting there bored, I saw a book on a shelf just below the countertop. The book was about the life of Edgar Cayce. He had some clairvoyant abilities that allowed him to diagnose people's medical issues with amazing accuracy by putting himself into a state of hypnosis. He was a strong Christian who did not believe in reincarnation. After listening to one of the recordings of himself in a state of hypnosis, he heard himself say that "reincarnation was an indisputable fact," which changed his entire philosophy of life. After reading that book, I was certainly glad that I had telephone duty on that day, which was the answer to my prayers. And, of course, by this time I was practicing Buddhism and a firm believer in that concept.

So, with that in mind I always wanted to have Ghanja with good eyesight. Therefore, when I picked out a puppy, I picked the one that looked most like Ghanja. I always fantasized that Oni (short for Onichi-Nyo, an historical figure in Nichiren Buddhism) was a reincarnation of Ghanja. There is no way for me to know if she was or wasn't, but it was great to have a dog that looked so much like Ghanja that had great eyesight. Oni was a great dog, good watch dog, loved kids and they loved her. She lived for ten years before she developed a stomach issue she could not overcome. I chanted in her ear as she took her last breath. As far as pets are concerned, she was a dream come true.

Oni (rest in peace puppy)

FNCC (Florida Nature and Culture Center)

FNCC was the brainchild of Daisaku Ikeda after the SGI split from Nichiren Shoshu and the priesthood, and we could no longer go on *tozan*, or our pilgrimage to the temple grounds.

FNCC is located near Fort Lauderdale, Florida. The campus grounds consist of several lodging facilities for, I think, about 180 conference participants, with a cafeteria, gymnasium, pool, library, and buildings with various exhibits pertaining to the history of SGI and the history of Nichiren Buddhism. It is a beautiful campus on the edge of a lagoon-type body of water with alligators, which to my knowledge no one has ever had a run-in with.

The first conference I attended at FNCC was for the Men's Division. I don't remember the year, but I remember running into some musicians, and we had the most incredible jam session in the cafeteria. I have been back several times, and it has always been a great place to grow in faith. At one conference I had the wonderful opportunity to sit down with the great jazz musician Wayne Shorter and pick his brain for about two hours. To me it was like magic, and I was hooked on FNCC. Later after Wayne Shorter's passing, that became a much more treasured experience to me.

I think the idea of attending a conference at FNCC, as well as with our former pilgrimages to Japan (or *tozan*), is to put forth a great effort in a reasonably short period of time that will allow you to experience an obvious growth in your life, and sometimes a major karmic breakthrough. For example, the first time I went on *tozan*, not only did I grow in faith, but on my return home my job suddenly changed from night shift to day shift, which I had desired desperately. These trips are always designed for the participants to have a great time while becoming more awakened to the teachings of Nichiren Daishonin.

Recently I was informed of our first Art's Department Conference since the pandemic, and of course I jumped at the opportunity to go. When I headed for the airport, Mildred, my wife, encouraged me to take advantage of any mobile transportation while traveling, since I had just had major surgery to remove a metal rod from the femur of my right leg while replacing my right knee in June of 2021, and I had a left knee replacement in March of 2022.

Normally there would be two participants in a room at FNCC, but because of the covid pandemic, there was only one person in a room, which meant the conference was half the size, about 90 participants. However, the energy of this conference was amazing. Immediately after every morning gongyo they would always play upbeat, energetic music. I think it was Sunday morning when the music started playing and everyone started dancing. A small energetic woman with silver colored hair grabbed me to dance. When I danced with her, she said," Oh! you can dance!" From that point on, when I would run into her, she would always refer to me as her dance partner. In any case, the music got so contagious that morning that we all formed a conga line and danced all around the auditorium.

The highlight of the conference for me was a lecture on "The Three Thousand Realms in a Momentary State of Existence" by Greg Martin, the senior leader for the conference. I also ran into a singer friend of mine and a bass player who I had shared some great jam sessions with, in past conferences, but we didn't have the opportunity to play together this time around. As a matter of fact, I never took my little soprano saxophone out of its case.

Most of my energy at this conference was spent walking and reading. I was going through one exhibit after another and trying so hard to understand and retain it all, that I felt almost dizzy. At one point I ran into an exhibit that had a television display and a bench in front of it. I sat down to watch the video and was so tired I started dozing. I couldn't stay there too long because I would have fallen asleep.

Although the conference was incredible, Monday morning came around very fast, and I had to leave for the airport. My transportation was leaving the campus at 9:00am. My flight left Fort Lauderdale at 11:00am and with a layover in Houston TX I arrived back in Phoenix at 2:20pm Monday, September 19. As I got off the plane a young man with a wheelchair said, "Do you need a ride?" I said, "No thank you." But I must have been a little shaky because he said, "Are you sure?" And I said, "Yes, I'm good." (As I thought about what Mildred had said.)

After returning to Phoenix, I think I may have experienced the most profound benefit on this trip than any other in the past. I had been practicing my saxophone daily for some time to keep my crippling hands from getting worse. Or so I thought. Lately I realized it is way more profound than that. The desire to play music comes from way down deep inside of me. I have dreamed of easily playing music from since I was a child, and was playing piano, ukulele and drums before I was 12. In reflecting on musical child prodigies like Mozart and others, it became clear that these young prodigal musicians must have had a head start over most people. Combining that thought with all the intense study at the conference, my confidence in the Buddhist concept on the eternity of life soared. I realized that I was not practicing for my hands, but rather to fulfill my mission in this life, and even more important, my life beyond this life. When I practice now it's like when I was 19 years old, practicing on the flute and dreaming to become a great musician, but with way more focus and foresight. Today, when I practice both my music and my Buddhism, I am looking more into the future, the life beyond this life, and I think I am more optimistic than ever before, I am certain I will be a great musician in a future existence, and that makes me happy at this present moment.

Nichiren Daishonin: *"Make every possible effort for the sake of your next life. What is most important is that, by chanting Nam-myoho-renge-kyo alone, you can attain Buddhahood. It will no doubt depend on the strength of your faith. To have faith is the basis of Buddhism."* (The Real Aspect of the Gohonzon Written to Nichinyo on August 23, 1277, WND-1, 832)

Chapter V
The Way, I see It Now!

Mic and Mac / Does size ready matter?

For the sake of clarification, I will refer the conglomerate of observable stars, galaxies, nebula, and other matter observable to humanity which is what they are usually referring to when they speak of "the big bang theory" as the "universe," and the space and anything potentially beyond that and beyond what we are able to observe in the microcosm as the "ultimate universe."

In Buddhism it is not unusual to refer to *"time without beginning,"* so, whether you agree with the concept or not, let's take a closer look at the concept of eternity as well as infinity. From a religious point of view, I think most believers have no problem with thinking of their ultimate deity as being eternal, which reminds me of when I was a kid and asked my grandmother where God came from and her answer without hesitation was, "He has always been." It seems to me that science is always looking for a beginning. However, it is science that says that matter and energy can't be created or destroyed; they only change form. To me that indicates that they are eternal. The Buddhist concept of life or existence is exactly that. "… like King Ajātashatru, who became a follower of the Buddha, cured his white leprosy, and prolonged his life by forty years; though lacking the roots of faith, he reached the first stage of security, and in his present life gained the realization that phenomena neither are born nor perish." *Writings of Nichiren Daishonin vol.1, pg. 619 Written to lay priest Takahashi Between 1275 and 1280,* From the Gosho, "Many in Body, One in Mind."

Of course, speaking subjectively, the past and the future are both eternal, or without beginning or end and the center of it is always in the present. Realistically, both the past and the future exist only in the present. They exist only in our mind at the present. Space is a little different, even though they are similar from the viewpoint of the observer. The microcosm and the macrocosm are defined by the observer. Let's imagine the volume of our universe as defined by the Big Bang which is rapidly and constantly expanding at any given second. In that same second, imagine the volume of an atom of helium. Let's call the volume of the universe X and the volume of the helium atom Y. Let's imagine dividing X by Y, and we will call the quotient Z (X/Y=Z). Z would be a number most of us would not even know how to express. Now imagine dividing the atom by Z (Y/Z). Of course, you could do that infinitely and to my knowledge mankind has nothing to evaluate life at that level. Now imagine multiplying X (the volume of the universe), by Z, which would mean observing our universe like we would a helium atom. If we could observe life from that perspective, our entire universe would be less than an insignificantly observable speck in the ultimate universe. In both cases in the microcosm and the macrocosm you could repeat that concept an infinite number of times and come nowhere close to the end. That's what infinity looks like.

The thing about infinity is that no matter who you are or where you are, or what your status maybe you, are always in the center of it. In Buddhism you sometimes hear a reference to the *ten directions,* which should be interpreted as all the directions on a compass plus up and down. And, also, *the three existences* would be past, present, and future. Therefore, you are always in the center of the ten directions and the three existences, in both space and time.

The Big Step!

When I started this journey toward answering the question of "Mind over matter," it wasn't difficult to see how my mind could permanently affect my own body, because it was one living organism. with the mind being the control center of everything else, although much of the mind's function was subconscious. The biggest step I took spiritually or even toward religious thinking was when I came to realize that the entire earth was one big living organism and that this whole big living thing one might call the Ultimate Universe was one big living organism, all interconnected. Just like a plant, an animal, or all other living beings. I heard a report on the ozone layer that we had damaged some years back. After we became aware of it and started putting forth an effort to limit sulfur and carbonous aerosol emissions from supersonic aircraft and trying to cut back on so much aerosol usage in our daily environment, the more recent update is that the ozone layer is healing on its own, much like a layer of my skin might heal from some recent damage.

As I was thinking about it, I realized that this earth is alive just like each one of us who are a part of it, or even, one could say a microcosm of it. I remember how I was disappointed when I first read from Nichiren's writing where he said that we human beings were responsible for the calamities and misfortunes that we were experiencing was because of their incorrect teachings and living. To me at the time it sounded a lot like some of the things I had heard in church. However, after a while I began to hear things from the scientific community that sounded much the same. The truth is, it is all me and you and the earth and beyond, that are all *one big life.* When I look at things that way it is much easier for me to see how one would influence their environment. To come to the realization that the earth is one living entity is quite easy to perceive since we are all living on this one planet and we can watch all the living beings, both animal and vegetable, do their own thing while they are creating value for the whole planet, much like all the small cells in our own body. And if you think about it, all the mind power of all the animals—particularly human beings—Is also the mind power of this life, we call earth. Yes, this earth and everything beyond it is alive and one big organism. We human beings have not found anything like the concentration of flourishing life like this earth in our observable universe, but we have observed that the elements that make up our life here are the same as those of the sun and the other stars in our observable universe.

The Ultimate Universe and the Ultimate Diety

Soka Gakkai was originally founded in Japan in 1930. It was the brainchild of Tsunesaburo Makiguchi (1871-1944), who was the principal of the Shirokane Elementary School, and along with his young disciple and schoolteacher, Jōsei Toda (1900-1958), founded Soka Kyoiku Gakkai (Value-Creating Education Society). The official date of Soka Kyoiku Gakkai's birth is Noember.18, 1930. At that time it was primarily a group of educators. To express my opinion of the Ultimate Deity, I would like to start by sharing an experience of Jōsei Toda's.

Toda along with his mentor Makiguchi joined Nichiren Shoshu because Makiguchi felt that Nichiren Buddhism had the correct view on life from the perspective of his theory of "Value Creation," *(which I personally have come to believe is the most fundamental motivation of life)*. Here are his words in a 1935 pamphlet summarizing his educational theories, Makiguchi wrote*: "As my research into The System of Value-Creating Pedagogy advanced and I was preparing to publish the first volume, I was moved by chance to research the Lotus Sutra, and my attitude to religion underwent a profound transformation. ... I was astonished to discover that [the Lotus Sutra] in no way contradicted the scientific and philosophical principles which form the basis for our daily lives, and that it differed fundamentally from all religious and moral practices which I had studied to date. And just as I found myself moved by this discovery, I experienced a number of inexplicable phenomena in my daily life, which accorded precisely with the teachings of the Lotus Sutra... With a joy that is beyond the power of words to express, I completely renewed the basis of the life I had led for almost sixty years."*

As of 1939, World War II had broken out and at some point, the Japanese Government had decided that Japan should all unify under the Shinto religion and the emperor. On June 27, 1943, Makiguchi, Toda and six other directors of the Soka Kyoiku Gakkai were summoned to the head temple of Nichiren Shoshu at which time they were pressured to accept the Shinto talisman in support of the Shinto Religion and the Emperor's ideology, for the sake of unity of Japan. Makiguchi refused. On July 6, 1943, both Makiguchi and Toda were arrested on the charges of violating the *"Peace Preservation Law."* It should be noted that the Nichiren Shoshu Priesthood accepted the Shinto talisman from the Japanese authorities without hesitation.

Once Makiguchi and Toda were arrested, they experienced heavy interrogation. I'm sure that at the very beginning, Makiguchi was put through particularly harsh treatment since he was the oldest and the obvious leader of the two. However, with his age and health, the harsh treatment took its toll and after a little more than two years he passed away in prison on November 18, 1944, at a little more than 73 years of age. Ironically, he passed on the same date (November 18) that they had founded the Soka Kyoiku Gakkai.

In any case it was during Toda's stay in prison that he had what I would call his awakening. While he was in prison in that small solitary and dingy room, he was chanting about 10,000 daimoku (1 daimoku =1 Nam-myho-renge-kyo) daily, which was about two to three hours, depending on the speed at which he repeated Nam-myho-renge-kyo. He had read the entire Lotus Sutra several times but was struck by a difficult passage in the Virtuous Practices chapter of the Sutra of Immeasurable Meanings, which serves as an introduction to the Lotus Sutra. In the passage it was describing the entity of the life of the Buddha. Of course, being a mathematician it's hard for me to imagine him just blowing past this passage without understanding it. In Classical Chinese it was expressed in 34 characters or 34 negations. In English it was something like this, "His entity (the life of the Buddha) is:
Without cause or condition,
Without self, or others.
Neither Square nor round,

Neither short, nor long.
Without appearance or disappearance,
Without birth, or death.
Neither created, nor emanating,
Neither made nor produced.
Neither sitting nor lying,
Neither walking nor stopping.
Neither moving nor rolling,
Neither calm nor quiet;
Without advance or retreat,
Without safety or danger;
Without right or wrong,
Without merit or demerit;
Neither that nor this,
Neither going nor coming;
Neither blue nor a yellow,
Neither red nor white;
Neither crimson, nor purple,
Without a variety of color.

Basically, to me, the passage seemed to be saying that this entity is not necessarily, or immediately detected by our five senses, and yet is the entity of them all.

"Here is an excerpt from the original "Human Revolution" vol. 4, page 8. "He continued chanting daimoku, ceaselessly trying to come ever nearer to the true meaning of the "entity." He fell into a deep meditation, recalling each of the thirty-four negations one after the other, trying to imagine what it might be that could absolutely exist despite so many negational words. He was no longer conscious of the passing of time and completely forgot where he was.

*Suddenly, the word **"life"** flashed through his mind. And in that instant, he arrived at a complete awareness of the twelve mystic lines. (Keeping in mind that it doesn't work out very well in English). The entity of the Buddha was life itself.*

Before I continue, I must address the integrity, courage, and sincerity of the two educators who founded this lay organization. Makiguchi literally gave his life for his belief while Toda was released from prison in July 1945 and began rebuilding the organization as the Soka Gakkai dropping the "Kyoiku," making it appeal to more than just educators, as "The Value Creating Society." He was determined to fulfill his mentor's dream and did so with great success. Toda passed away on April 2, 1958, and 250,000 people attended his funeral service on April 20. Toda had a goal of 750,000 Soka Gakkai households of membership in Japan, which was realized by his disciple, Daisaku Ikeda, who was motivated by the determination to fulfill his mentor, Josei Toda's dream and became the President of the Soka Gakkai after Toda's passing.

So, based on Toda's awakening, and the only way I can see that science and religion could both be a reality, I would conclude that the Ultimate Deity would be life itself, or to be more exact, *the entity of life itself*. And where might that entity be? Well, it would be in every living being, which includes all animals and plants. But the most important place you would find the entity is within your own life, which I will elaborate on in greater detail. But first, let's look at life's entity as it spreads from one generation to another. In going from one generation to another life has three components. They are the *parent*, the *offspring* and **life** itself that is spread from the parent to the offspring. And that applies to both animals and vegetation. In Buddhism there is a concept called *"The Three Treasures."*

The Three Treasures

(Not to be confused with the three types of treasures, which are the treasures of the storehouse or material wealth, the treasures of the body, or physical health and the treasures of the heart which is more founded in living with wisdom.)

183

"The Three Treasures are the *"Buddha, the Dharma and the Sangha."* You could say the "Buddha" is "the wise one" or ultimate teacher; the Dharma, the ultimate law or teaching; and the Sangha is the community of believers. It is through this process, or "entity" of these three elements that the teaching spreads from one person to another and one generation to another. Life itself also has an "entity of three elements that allows it to spread in the same way. Those elements are called, parent, offspring, and life itself, which again fits the description of the "34 negatives" of Toda's awakening. It is also apparent in both animal and plant forms of life. Here is a passage from the *Writings of Nichiren Daishonin* (WND): *"All these things I have done solely to repay the debt I owe to my parents, the debt I owe to my teacher, and the debt I owe to the three treasures of Buddhism, and the debt I owe to my country. For their sake I have been willing to destroy my body and to give up my life, though as it turns out, I have not been put to death after all." (WND, vol.1 pg.728 On Repaying Debts of Gratitude" Written to Joken-bo and Gijo-bo on July 21, 1276)*

In this passage written by Nichiren, he touches on the concept of the Three Treasures on three levels, that of the family, the arena of education or learning and of the society or country. It is said that the Buddha has the three attributes of parent, teacher, and sovereign. That would be one who has the compassion, love, and protective qualities of a parent, one who has the wisdom, knowledge, and skills of a great teacher and the wisdom and the ability to care for an entire society or country.

In looking back on my life as a child in the Christian community, I can't help seeing the similarity of the trinity and the Three Treasures. However, all the explanations of its meaning I heard at the time I was a kid in church, were considerably different from all the explanations I have heard from the Buddhist teachings. But parent, offspring, and life, or Mentor, Disciple and Teaching, sure sounds a lot like "Father, Son and Holy Spirit," especially since Christianity today is a lot like early forms of Buddhism.

In early Buddhism there were lots of commandments, or precepts, as many as 500 for women and 250 for men (I will address the discrepancy between sexes later). But the thing I would address first was the deities of India and the early Asian communities. There were many of those deities, way more than I can address. However, the most important thing I would address here is the fact that they were all outside oneself. The word Buddha literally means, "The Awakened One" or "Teacher." The one person usually considered the original historical Buddha was Siddhartha Gautama, also known as Shakyamuni, who was a prince of the Shakya Klan. I would say in the Asian community, Shakyamuni's life is usually estimated between 600 and 1,000 BCE. while in the western community maybe somewhere between 100 and 600 BCE. In any case, in the concept of the Three Treasures, the most important relationship is between the Buddha and the Sangha, as in all of living beings where it would be the parent and the offspring or in any teaching, teacher and student. In SGI, the most important relationship in spreading our movement based on Nichiren Buddhism, is that of mentor and disciple. It is only through the oness or unity of that relationship and the unity of the believers that *kosen rufu*, or world peace can be achieved.

The Ten Worlds

Some early Buddhists taught that if one follows these commandments, one might be reborn in the Buddha land of perfect bliss in the west or the Medicine Masters pure emerald world in the east. Here is a quote from Nichiren, *"First of all, as to the question of where exactly hell and the Buddha exists, one sutra states that hell exists underground, and another sutra says that the Buddha is in the west. Closer examination, however, reveals that both exist in our five-foot body. This must be true because hell is in the heart of a person who inwardly despises his father and disregards his mother. It is like the Lotus seed, which contains both blossom and fruit. In the same way the Buddha dwells within our hearts." (WND,1137) New Year's Gosho Written to the wife of Omosu on January 5, year unknown.*

Of course, we know Nichiren lived in the 13th century. The point here is that early Buddhism was describing places like the Buddha Land and Hell as existences outside themselves, much like Christianity was taught to me as a kid, which, as I grew older, became impossible for me to believe. In Nichiren Buddhism there is a concept called the Ten Worlds which are ten different categories, life conditions or states of mind that each of us toggle through daily. However, at one point it was thought that these ten worlds were ten different places you would experience. The term is called," The mutual possession of the Ten Words" because as human beings we are aways in at least one of those ten life conditions, from Hell at the lowest to Buddhahood at the highest. The Ten Worlds are (1) the world of hell or a state of complete misery (2) the world of hunger, a state of unsatiable desire (3) the world animality, (a condition driven by instinct without wisdom, reason, or morality, "dog eat dog" (4) the world of asuras or anger (5) the world of human beings, the normal state of human beings, maybe tranquility (6) the world of heavenly beings (rapturous) (7) the world of voice-hearers (one the learns the fundamental realities of life from one's predecessors and contemporaries). (8) the world of cause-awakened ones (one who awakens to the fundamental realities of life through their own experience). (9) the world of bodhisattvas (one who dedicates his life for the happiness of all others). 1 through 6 are called the six paths and are usually considered the paths most people toggle through throughout their lives. The people who transmigrate between these six worlds is also called the "threefold world." (10) The world of Buddhas or Buddhahood. This is the state of absolute freedom when one realizes the true state of all phenomena. In a letter to Toki Jonin, Nichiren Daishonin wrote," Buddhahood is the most difficult to demonstrate," (WND vol 1 p. 358) so for now I will leave it there. The main point is that all the words like hell, heaven, and Buddha lands that we experience before and after death, are experienced right here in this mundane existence.

Three Thousand Realms in a Momentary State of Existence

To better elucidate life's entity lets address, "Ichinen Sanzen," which is a conceptual teaching originally developed by the great Chinese teacher, T'ien-tai (538-597) which I think of as the dissecting of the "life moment."

The word "ichinen" is one of my favorite Japanese words. It can be translated as one thought, one mind or one thought moment. In any goal, a lot depends on that initial moment of determining the goal, and how strong of a determination there was in that moment. So, the foundation of the term is based on "the ten worlds," which range all the way from our absolute worst experience to our absolute best experience, at any given moment. In each of these ten worlds there is always the potential to go into any of the ten at the next moment. The ten worlds' times their potential worlds are how we arrive at 100 possible conditions or realms.

Then there are the ten factors, which are (1) appearance: attributes that can be discernible from the outside, such as color, form shape, etc. (2) nature: the inherent quality of a thing or being that cannot be discerned from the outside. (3) entity: the essence of life that permeates and integrates appearance and nature. (4) power: life's potential energy. (5) influence: the action or movement produced when life's inherent power is activated. (6) internal cause: the cause latent in life that produces an effect of the same quality as itself, that is, good evil or neutral. (7) relation: the relationship of the indirect causes to the internal cause. Internal causes are various conditions, both internal and external, that help the internal cause produce an effect. (8) latent effect: the effect produced in life when an internal cause is activated through its relationship with various conditions. (9) Manifest effect: the tangible perceiv-

187

able result that emerges in time as an expression of a latent effect and therefore of an internal cause, again through its relationship with various conditions. (10) Their consistency from beginning to end: the unifying factor between all the other factors, which means that whatever of the ten worlds you're in at any given moment, will be reflected or expressed in the ten factors and the "Three Realms of Existence."

The Three Realms of Existence are (1) The realm of the five components, which are form, perception, conception, volition, and consciousness. Form includes everything that constitutes the body and its sense organs, through which one perceives the outer world. Perception means the function of receiving or apprehending external information through one's sense organs. Conception indicates the function by which one grasps and forms some idea or concept about what is being perceived. Consciousness is the cognitive function of discernment that integrates the components of perception. (2) The realm of living beings: The individual formed of a temporary union of the five components, who manifests or experiences any of the Ten Words. The realm of living beings refers to an individual as an integrated whole, but since no living being exist in perfect isolation, it is also taken to mean the collective body of individuals who interact with one another. (3) The realm of the environment: The place or land where living beings' dwell and carry out life activities. The state of the land is a reflection of the state of life of the people who live in it. You might say, (2) who you are, (3) where you are (1) and the analyzation of your subjective experience at any given moment or instant.

So, all the ten worlds with the potential of all the other ten worlds in them equals 100, and are experienced through the ten factors, equaling one thousand, and all this is experienced through "the three realms of existence." So, that's how we arrive at three thousand realms.

At one point I tried to imagine or analyze how I experienced the "three thousand realms" in the moments I experienced my horrific accident in 1991. The thing that stood out first the moment of fear I experienced when the car just to the right of me, not realizing I was in his blind spot, turned into me and forced me into oncoming traffic. Of course, the immediate feeling was the instant fear of uncertainty, and in that instant all the "three thousand realms" I was experiencing reflected the world of hell I was in from that fear. However, after the crash, in the next moment I remember experiencing a clear feeling of gratitude realizing I was still alive. However, after a quick assessment, I saw my bone sticking out of my leg, which changed my life condition considerably. Of course, that day I went through a lot of ups and downs, until later the day when the surgeon came out and said I had about an eighty percent chance of recovery. However, you're always experiencing the complexities of the "three thousand realms" even with a simple experience like smelling the sweet fragrance of a rose, even though it is a much more pleasant experience.

The Nine Consciousnesses

For me, probably this most clarifying Buddhist concept that helped me feel my oneness with the whole ultimate universe was the Buddhist concept of the "Nine Consciousnesses." **The first five consciousnesses are our five senses**, sight, hearing, taste. touch and smell. **The sixth consciousness** is what I think of as our immediately conscious mind that integrates our five senses in a way that makes sense or is coherent to us. I think one could say it is the part of our mind that we are most aware of. Even independent of our first five consciousnesses, our sixth consciousness is used while dreaming and with our imagination. I think that consciousness is what we most think about when we think of our mind. Then there is the **seventh or mano-consciousness,** that is the consciousness that modern psychology would call the ego. This is the consciousness that recognizes oneself as an individual. It is in this level of consciousness that, in my humble opinion, that we should be most cautious. I have seriously practiced two religions in my lifetime: one was Christianity and the other is Buddhism, which is my current practice. In Christianity there was the character Lucifer or Satan, in historical Buddhism, there is a character called *"Dai Rokuten no Mao."* Which translates from Japanese to English as "Great or King Devil of the Sixth Heaven," which resides in the highest or the sixth heaven of desires. In any case, to me, all these guys represent the ultimate bad guy or evil. In Christianity Lucifer was considered the fallen angel because he was originally from heaven and fell into hell because of his behavior, and Dai Rokuten, Devil king of the sixth heaven, I think are both mythological characters that represent the potential of evil or selfish nature we all have in our lives originally.

There is the question however, of why it is necessary to have these evil forces in our fundamental lives, these forces that are always pushing back on every positive and productive thing we do. There is a saying in the community of those who frequently exercise and work out, that says "No pain, no gain." The idea here is that if one does not push themselves beyond their comfort zone, they will not experience any real growth. The same is true in every aspect of life, without overcoming push-back one will never grow. "The faster you go, the greater the wind resistance." By overcoming the push-back, we all experience from the forces represented by the selfish nature within each of us as represented by these mythological characters, we become stronger and better human beings. So, the purpose of push-back of all evil desires is to give us the opportunity to become stronger, and live happier lives.

Overcoming obstacles is always the way to all true success. I think that from the point of view of the seventh consciousness, we are not necessarily aware of any level of consciousness beyond that. The problem with that way of thinking is that there is no mechanism in place to prevent one from seeking one's own desires at the expense of someone else's loss. It seems to me that humanity too much of the time looks at this vast universe as this big dumb thing which we as intelligent human beings in our microcosm are a part of, just as I did. It seems to never occur to us that the universe or life itself may be infinitely more intelligent than we are individually since we are a microcosm of it.

The **eighth or alaya-consciousness** is the level of consciousness where all our deeds, both good and evil, which we call our karma, are stored. One could refer to the eighth consciousness as our karma storage. Of course, good causes are those causes one makes in support of life and bad causes are those made against life's progress, both good and bad causes toward oneself and others and life in general. The eighth consciousness is like the memory hard drive where nothing is ever lost. Of course, groups like families, communities and nations will more directly share this consciousness because of the causes and effects they share together. Of course, since we are on this planet together, we share some karma and therefore that level of consciousness.

And then there is the **ninth or amala-consciousness,** which we all also share. *"The ninth consciousness is itself the ultimate reality of all things and is equivalent to the universal Buddha nature. Buddhism teaches that we can change our deepest karma through drawing upon this inner capacity of our lives rather than through the intervention of an external god"(Unlocking the Mysteries of Birth and Death* by Daisaku Ikeda, p. 162) To me, if life was like a tree, the ninth consciousness would be like the heart or core of the tree trunk that connects directly to the heart and core of every little branch and twig. And of course, that consciousness is shared by all. One could say that the nineth consciousness is our Buddha nature that we all can access and is the foundation of all. *"Tapping our inner wisdom, compassion and life force is crucial. The full value of the nine consciousnesses concept is demonstrated only when one practically brings forth the ninth*

consciousness, or Buddhahood". (Unlocking the Mysteries of
Birth and Death, p.)

From the point of view of our modern psychology, the only thing I can think of that is like our sharing levels of consciousness as in sharing the eight and ninth levels in Buddhism, would be Carl Jung's (Swiss psychiatrist, 1865-1961) theories on the Collective Unconsciousness.

For me, in realizing this inner connection, it becomes extremely important to strengthen my expressions of gratitude, appreciation, compassion and all tangible connections we have with others and everything around us (me). One of those tangible connections is "responsibility." ***"Who is responsible for the protection and care of this whole infinite existence?"*** **That would be me, or more specifically, that would be oneself.**

As we realize this oneness of all that exists, we come to realize that we are responsible for it all. In all cases win or lose it is all up to us (me/you). When we can look past the limitations of identifying ourselves from the perspective of our egos (the seventh consciousness) and begin to identify ourselves from the perspective of all of life in its macrocosm as one, based on the ninth consciousness, this is what Buddhism calls, **"The Greater Self,"** as opposed to looking at oneself from the perspective of the ego, or the **"The Lesser Self."**

The Strict Law of "Cause and Effect"
Isaac Newton's Third Law: Action & Reaction-
His third law states that for every action (force) in nature there is an equal and opposite reaction. If object A exerts a force on object B, object B also exerts an equal and opposite force on object A. In other words, forces result from interactions.
The above is what I have always thought of when I heard the term "cause and effect." And, I guess I have always thought of

it as being very fundamental. Of course, the equal and opposite may be a little confusing, but equal refers to the nature and intensity, and opposite refers to the direction (the cause is outgoing, and the effect is incoming). I did not however, see it so strictly as to relate it to human interaction such as morality. In my mind it was simply a law of physics. However, I have come to see it as a law that's more fundamental in every aspect of life. After all, if I intentionally ignore a loved one at a crucial moment, that might be a cause with little or no physical action in its effect, that could however, bring about a devastating effect that's not necessarily in the physical realm. So, with living beings the "cause and effect" principal is not always a physical action and can still be very real and complicated.

In general, I had always thought of this vast universe as a big unintelligent conglomerate of matter. However, there is that little thing that we refer to as life. Here on our planet earth, we see a very sophisticated, harmonious, and interactional display between animal, vegetable, gasses, minerals etc., that is, at the very least evidence of a vast amount of intelligence.

It was at this point on May 28, 2023, which was one day after I had written the sentence just above this, that I was not sure what to say next, so, after reciting a portion of the Lotus Sutra, and chanting Nam-myoho-renge-kyo for one hour, which is my normal daily practice these days, I had what one might call an epiphany. As I was trying to figure out how to express the significance of the law of cause and effect, I realized that nothing could possibly exist without a cause, and that existence is, an effect, therefore, the law of cause and effect is the fundamental law of all existence. Nothing could exist without it, on any level. And that is exactly the point, there is no such thing as existence on any level or in any dimension without that law. All causes we make as human beings will either create value or anti-value. That is the way of existence, whether animate or inanimate. Which brings me to the Buddhist concept of the "three poisons."

The Three Poisons

The three poisons in Buddhism are an example of anti-value, as in greed, anger, and stupidity (or foolishness). I think it is obvious that the one species on this planet Earth that has the greatest influence on the planet is humanity. Like it or not, we can make or break the quality of life on, and of, this earth. Again, I think it is important for us to remember that each of us are microcosms of the macrocosm of the earth and indeed the entire ultimate universe. For me the Golden Rule comes to mind: "to do unto others as you would have them do unto you." In realizing our oneness with the community, the earth, and the universe, our actions to protect all of it should be perfectly clear. The three poisons are three common things we should avoid. **Greed** of course can lead to an unhealthy distribution of wealth and other needs; **anger** can lead to war and conflicts that have been so devastating in our history and **stupidity/foolishness** leads to pestilence etc. which have presented major horrific circumstances in our human history.

I think it is quite clear how prevalent these three poisons have already been in our history as human beings. Of course, I think these human shortcomings are a result of our constantly perceiving ourselves as individuals with no real or fundamental connection to one another, or not seeing beyond our seventh level of consciousness. However, when we all began to look at things from the point of view of the Greater Self, we come to realize that everything and everyone we harm is only harm we are doing to ourselves. I cannot stress the oneness of ourselves and our surroundings enough. Becoming aware of that fact was probably the greatest step I have taken toward achieving wisdom and understanding.

My Daily Practice

Fundamentally, life operates in a repetitive continuum of particles and waves on many different levels. I guess you could say particles represent building blocks of the matter or energy involved, and waves represent the process. From the perspective of our daily life let's examine the wave process. The wave has two extremes, the crest and trough. The crest is the high point or the peak and the trough the low point or the valley. When I picture a wave in the ocean, I picture a wave moving up out of the water and when it reaches its high point or crest, it seems to run out of energy and fall back down, then the weight and velocity of the water coming back down will determine the height of the next wave. Of course, this is all determined by an external factor like the wind or some other factor determining the motion and speed of the water. Each wave's height is determined by the amount of force or energy that created it. And of course, it always runs out of energy at its crest and creates more energy at the trough from the water compression created from the previous wave. I'm sure that a scientist could do a much better job explaining this, but the point I'm trying to make here is that it seems to have the characteristics expending energy in the crest and rejuvenation in the trough.

When we go to sleep at night, we rejuvenate our bodies and during the day we expend energy and then we must rest or rejuvenate ourselves again. When we breathe in and out during the day, each breath is a form of expending energy and rejuvenating. When you breathe in that's a form of rejuvenation and when we breathe out that is expending energy. Even when our heart beats, each beat is a process of pumping the blood through and rejuvenating for the next pump. My daily practice is in rhythm with that same process. After I get up and do my personal stuff like shower and get dressed, I do the practice of gongyo. Gongyo means assiduous practice in Japanese and is a recitation of key parts of the Lotus Sutra, (portions of the second and sixteenth chapter) we as

SGI members use as part of our daily practice, and then we chant the phrase, Nam-myoho-renge-kyo. To recite that phrase one time is called one daimoku, or literally one "prayer." Chanting that phrase is considered our essential practice while reciting gongyo is considered our supporting practice. Nam-myoho-renge-kyo is the essence of gongyo and indeed, the essence of the entire Lotus Sutra. Usually, one would recite gongyo and then at the end of gongyo chant daimoku (*Nam myoho renge kyo*) as long as you would like or have time for.

As Nichiren says," *The true perfect teaching practice is to keep the mouth constantly reciting Nam-myoho-renge-kyo, whatever the occasion, and to keep the mind fixed on the meditation on the three thousand realms in a single moment of life. This is the practice and understanding of persons of wisdom. For the ordinary lay believers of Japan, however, it is sufficient if they concentrate solely on the recitation of Nam-myoho-renge-kyo. ("On the Five Seasonal Festivals, (WND Vol II pg379 Written to Akimoto Taro (1271))* Usually in the mornings when I do gongyo or my morning practice, I am more energetically focused on having a productive day and for my evening gongyo its more a spirit of winding down.

The general definition of Nam-myoho-renge-kyo is as follows. Namu, comes from the Sanskrit word *namas*, meaning "devotion," and usually when it is followed by a word beginning with the letter "M," the "U" is dropped. Nam is an affirmation of your commitment to something and Myoho means "mystic law." "Renge" means cause and effect, and Kyo means sutra or teaching.

Myo or Mystic, meaning it's not easily comprehended, and law or ho is the law that governs everything. It has been said that myoho is nether existent nor non-existent but has the characteristics of both. Be that as it may, you could say one can't see, feel, or touch it; however, it is at the foundation of everything. Also, myo represents death, and ho represents life. Since Buddhism believes in the eternity of life, each life is but another example of the wave concept, as I described above, in our eternal existence. Myo also means "to revive," which also corresponds with the "rejuvenation stage" of the wave, and of course ho would be compared to the "expending energy stage," because eventually one must rest or "rejuvenate." To continue to move forward. (*Living beings that pass through the two phases of life and death are the entities of the Ten Worlds, or the entities of Myoho-renge-kyo. WND 1, p.216*) Buddhism believes that there is no form of life that is free from those two stages of life and death. That is the continual process of life.

Renge is the name of the lotus flower which is uniquely known as a flower that produces its blossom and seeds simultaneously, which emphasizes the simultaneity of cause and effect. At the most fundamental point the cause and effect are always simultaneous, which is at the very point the cause becomes the effect. One could say that at the instant the cause is made, the effect is inherently there, simultaneously.

Kyo in its original Chinese character translates as "warp," as in the warp or foundation or vertical or length threads of a woven fabric. In Japanese, with phrases like, "The voice does the Buddha's work", along with the fundamental relationship of the voice and sound and the fact that most of the teaching was spread that way, it is not difficult to see how that at one-point kyo was defined as vibrations. The important thing here, I think, is to always be looking, learning from, and observing the most fundamental aspect of life. That, I think, is the great successful nature of the quantum sciences, and that is the heart of the Lotus Sutra, and Nichiren Buddhism. The idea here is to embrace and take on all responsibility, with all your being, the essence and entity of all of life in its macrocosm, which you can find in its entirety, in the microcosm of your own life. That entity/essence is, Myoho-renge-kyo.

From the very first day I filled out an application for my Gohonzon (the Nichiren mandala and object of devotion), I chanted daimoku (Nam-myoho-renge-kyo) every day, which was August 13, 1971. At that time in Chicago there was no Nichiren Shoshu temple, so we had to wait approximately six months for the priest to come to town to receive a Gohonzon. As I mentioned earlier, I received my Gohonzon on February 27,1972. It was at that time I determined to never miss gongyo, and I have not. That does not mean that by missing gongyo that is the end of the world, but that was my choice, and today that means a lot to me.

To me, chanting Nam-myoho-renge-kyo, is the ultimate form of meditation for many reasons, but the two things that come to mind right away are that it elucidates the entity and essence of life itself which I think is the ultimate focal point of any meditation seeking awakening, and because it is so conducive to doing in a group setting, in other words, chanting together with others. I think this is important because we should always be aware that we are all individually a microcosm of this universal existence and the more we unite the better off we, as individuals, and the whole macrocosm will be.

There were years when I chanted Nam-myoho-renge-kyo three hours a day. That was probably the time when I made the greatest advance toward the more than 37,000,000 daimoku, (and still growing,) that I have chanted until today. However, recently, I have chosen to chant one hour, study for one hour and try to write for one hour.

The Gohonzon

The Ultimate Deity I would define as the essence or entity of life itself, is the "sometimes difficult to perceive law of cause and effect," or Myoho. The closest and most perceivable place of observation lies only within oneself, the entity of your own life since it exists in every life entity in the microcosm and the macrocosm. A mandala is the thing one would focus on while trying to perceive that entity. To me the Gohonzon is the ultimate mandala. Although the actual Gohonzon as the ultimate deity lies only within your life, the Gohonzon as a mandala I can describe. The whole idea was to share the enlightenment of Shakyamuni, the historical Buddha, with the rest of all humanity. This is done through what is referred to as the "Ceremony in the Air." "The Ceremony in the Air" was the second of three assemblies described in the Lotus Sutra between the "Treasure Tower," (eleventh chapter) and the "Entrustment" (twenty-second chapter). The other two assemblies were on "Eagle Peak." In the "Encouraging Devotion" (chapter thirteen, which is the chapter that resonates with me because of the number 13) it describes where "innumerable bodhisattvas attending the assembly vow to fulfill the Buddha's will even if they had to endure the three powerful enemies, which were arrogant lay people, arrogant priests and arrogant false or pretend sages. I would say the vow to fulfill the Buddha's will to make all human beings as enlightened as he was, no matter at what personal cost.

A tower or stupa adorned with treasures and jewels is not unique in any one Buddhist passage, but probably the most famous one was the treasure tower described in the "Treasure Tower" chapter (11th chapter) of the Lotus Sutra. It described this great tower of Many Treasures Buddha, 250 yojanas wide and 500 yojanas tall emerging from beneath the earth and is suspended in midair, with seven kinds of jewels and seated inside the tower was Many Treasures Buddha. Shakyamuni, after summoning the Buddhas, which were his emanations from the ten directions, stations himself in midair opens and enters the treasure tower and sits next to Many Treasures. "Then Shakyamuni through his transcendental powers lifts the entire assembly into space so that they are all on the same level." Now, always keep in mind that this is all coming from the life of Shakyamuni. I don't know whether it was a dream, vision or what his state of life was, but it came from his life. The only time I had a clear picture of the future before it happened was in a dream, so to me dreams are just another medium by which the truth can be revealed.

In the Ceremony in the Air, as well as on the Gohonzon as a mandala, are expressed certain realities in fundamental life that are not readily recognized. Right off the bat, Shakyamuni, seeing the emergence of the Treasure Tower in which Many Treasures Buddha was seated, then enters the tower and joins Many Treasures. This action of Shakyamuni, the observer and Many Treasures being the observed, indicates the fusion or oneness of subjective wisdom and objective reality, which is becoming more and more an accepted reality in our modern thinking. After all, there is no reality without the observer. I remember when I first looked up the word "realize" the definition was, "to bring into existence." In any case the Gohonzon as a mandala is based on this clearly described realization of Shakyamuni, the original historical Buddha.

When we do our daily practice (gongyo) we are reliving and participating in the Ceremony in the Air. The heart of the Gohonzon, as a mandala and the Treasure Tower is Nam myoho renge kyo written vertically down the middle. Keep in mind that it is our daily practice, and I think, the ultimate form of meditation because every step of the way and every character on the Gohonzon is a teachable expression of the fundamental nature of life.)

Now, since it is a ceremony, Shakyamuni and Many Treasures are at the front of the ceremony facing us, the congregation, which is me (us). However, from their point of view Shakyamuni is sitting on the right and Many Treasures on the left. Of course, from our perspective as part of the congregation, (which is us) Many Treasures is on our right and Shakyamuni is on our left. On either side of Shakyamuni and Many Treasures are the four Bodhisattvas of the Earth who were the leaders of the innumerable Bodhisattvas mentioned in the 21st chapter of the Lotus Sutra. "Superior Practices" which is just to the right of Many Treasures, and the leader of all the Bodhisattvas is believed to be Nichiren because of his life fulfilling the predicted criteria such as being banned three times and being struct with staves. He was struck by the very same scroll where that prediction existed. To the right of that is Boundless Practices. On our left of Shakyamuni are Firmly Established Practices and Pure Practices. The four Bodhisattvas also represent "the four virtues of a Buddha." From left to right they are "Happiness, Purity, True Self and Eternity." It has been said that Buddha is our original state. If that is the case, chanting to the Gohonzon is a way of awakening to that reality. We can also look at these four characteristics as our personal goals of 1) becoming happy, 2) developing a pure unshakable practice, 3) discovering our true selves as buddhas/bodhisattvas and 4) realizing the true infinite and eternal nature of life.

On the outer four corners of the Gohonzon are the four Great Heavenly Kings mentioned in the Lotus Sutra who vow to protect the practitioners of the Lotus Sutra. From our perspective, in the upper left corner is Dai Bishamon-Tenno, who is said to reside down the north side of Mount Sumeru and on the upper right is Dai Jikoku-Tenno, which is said to reside down the eastern side of Mount Sumeru and the lower left is Dai Zojo Tenno, who resides down the south side of Mount Sumeru and on the lower right is Dai Komoku-Tenno who resides down the western side of Mount Sumeru. These Heavenly Kings or Guardians represent the protection from all four directions, or more specifically, "the ten directions," for the practitioners of the Lotus Sutra. In bold text vertically down the center from the top is Nam-myoho-renge-kyo. On either side of this are deities that were originally Indian mythology, most notably Taishaku originally Shakra or Indra in India and Bonten or originally Brahma in India. To me, the point that is being made here is the message that we should embrace the law, which is the true deity of all that exists, from within our own lives. And that by embracing this law we will have the full protection from all corners of the universe, which I think is the ultimate mandala. Of course, always keeping in mind that the Gohonzon in its reality lies only within your own life and life itself extends outward infinitely.

Mildred Today

As mentioned earlier, Mildred and I first worked together as a team in the Buddhist organization NSA (Nichiren Shoshu of America), which of course later became SGI (Soka Gakkai International). Since that time, as described earlier, we were fortunate enough to have successfully raised two kids into two successful adults in the community. Since Mildred's father's death in 2012, and because of her mother's poor health, her mother "Red," came to live with us so Mildred could care for her. Since that time, with Red now being over 95 years old, she is totally dependent on Mildred for her survival. Red was an excellent cook in her day, and I think Mildred inherited her skills. And I have been reaping the benefits of that in the last, more than forty years. Which, as I said before, is one of the major reasons for my improved health in my senior years. I could never express enough gratitude for that.

When our first child, our daughter, was born, the very first time our daughter woke up and cried, I saw a response from Mildred that I had never seen before. There was no hesitation, the response was immediate. It was more immediate than I had ever seen her react to anything. I was thoroughly impressed, and I thought then, this is what it's like to be a mother.

Today, she still gets up early in the morning, a trait I think she got from her dad. Most of the years we have been together she would get up and go out for her morning walk. In our more recent senior years, she is not necessarily out walking as in her younger years, but she is up and chanting before I get out of bed. And, as part of her daily routine, she feeds the birds in the neighborhood. If she is late, I've seen the birds gather before she gets there with the bird food as if to hurry her up.

I say without hesitation, she was and is the heart of our family. I am reminded of the passage in the writings of Nichiren, when says, "A man is like the wings of a bird, a woman like the body. If the wings and the body become separated, then how can the bird fly?" (Written in1280) to lay Nun Sennichi, the wife of Abutsu-bo, WND 1 pg. 1043. Mildred is definitely the body (of the bird) in our household. And I hope that I am the wings. For the most important thing is he oness of the wings and the body.

The Clear Benefits of My Practice

Recently, I decided to get a dark blue dress suite, which was something that I had been planning to get for some time. I had felt that there may be some occasions that my one grey dress suite might not be so appropriate. Because I am small in stature, it is not easy for me to find some clothes that fit me well in most men's depts or men's clothing stores. So, I went to JCPenney's, a store where I have an account. They can usually fit me in the boy's department, but the only thing they had in junior sizes were to bright blue. However, in the men's dept. they had the exact color and material that I liked. So, when I went back a week later, I was determined to find a suite my size. Even if I had to convince them to order a junior size in the same material that I liked. I think I had convinced myself that I could achieve that. When I arrived at JCPenney's and found my way to the department that had the boy's suites, I happened to see a small dark blue suite hanging all alone, by itself as if someone had just looked at it and hung it on the first available place and walked away. When I asked about the suite and tried it on, it fitted perfectly except for a little adjustment with the sleeves and pants lengths. It took me about five minutes to buy that suite and I immediately went to a tailor for the minor alterations. Even the belt that I was wearing at the time, had come into my life through an almost identical experience. Those kinds of things happen to me enough that I genuinely always feel that someone or something, always has my back. Oh yes, I had ordered some black suspenders to go with my dark blue suite thinking that black would a safe choice rather than trying to match the suite, however, when the suspenders arrived and I pulled them out of the package they looked black, but when I saw them under better lighting the fabric portion of the suspenders were actually the exact color as my suite.

However, as I have described earlier, my understanding of the truth of how life really works was of major importance to me. The contradiction between science and the religious thinking I was exposed to as a kid was just not working for me. It seemed to me that I was asked to believe in a fantasy world. Today, just seeing the world through the eyes I have developed through my daily practice of Nichiren Buddhism, is far better than any utopia that I have ever seen described. <u>The realization that the entity of all life is to be found within me as it is in all living beings, is a clear answer to so very many of the questions I have had all my life. The joy of that realization alone is immeasurable.</u> For me, just being aware of that fact alone is completely liberating. The most important thing I must do is to make sure that everyone knows we are all one live existence and start functioning with the understanding that <u>protecting all of life is in fact protecting oneself</u>. When I see the flowers grow from a tiny seed, all animals and plants coming from their parents shows me all life is exploding from the inside. When I think of that, I do sometimes think of the "Big Bang." I think it must be part of a repetitious process with the characteristics of "expending energy and rejuvenating," as in that of a wave. I guess that is a question science is still working on. In any event, just seeing life in this way, and always growing and expanding my awareness is a tremendous adventure. And yes, I do have a much clearer understanding of the "mind over matter" concept, which was my first motivating question when I began this journey toward my enlightenment. My thirst for reading and learning has grown incredibly. Before I graduated high school, I had finished only one book, "The Great Expectations," by Charles Dickens, and 'til this day I don't really remember the point of the book. Today I read at least an hour a day and consider it as another form of meditation. And my health, I have not taken any medication for my rheumatoid arthritis in over a year, which is the longest I have gone without medication for R.A. since I was a kid. After seeing my rheumatologists recently, together, we decided to hold off on the medication until I really needed it. A short time ago I started getting a flare-up in my right ankle. At first, I began thinking about what medication I might start taking. Then I started thinking I should not be so excepting of the necessity to have to take medication so quickly. Instead, I decided to not let it come back into my life without a fight. Through my intense chanting I pumped up my fighting spirit and decided I would not let the flare up come back, and like a little whimpering dog it went away. However, about a day or so later it began coming back. After observing my attitude and the response I received, I decided to fight it at all costs. At this point I am winning the battle just as I am in all of life. This is an example of how life's obstacles never stop coming, however it is through one's relentless spirit to continue moving forward, no matter what, that is the path to your enlightenment. *(The greater the hardship befalling him, the greater the delight he feels, because of his strong faith . . . without tribulation there would be no votary of the Lotus Sutra. (WND 1, 33), A Ship to Cross the Sea of Suffering, Written to Shiiji Shiro on April 28, 1261),* my life at this point is like a great novel to me, that I am constructing as I experience it. I think this is what my mentor, Ikeda Sensei means when he keeps reminding us that we are the protagonist of our lives. Sometimes I think of my life like a movie, and my theme song is an old song that Bing Crosby use to sing called, "Pennies from Heaven," describing the rain, which is many times seen as an obstacle, is really bringing fortune into our lives. That is the theme of my life! When I practice my saxophone in the evenings, I usually play that song at some point.

I have had my share of adversity in my life, not the least of which was my lifetime struggle with R. A. which was possibly my greatest motivator for finding happiness through a path of understanding life at its depths. Without that motivation, I am confident that I would have been content with going throughout life, experiencing rapture at every available opportunity without any long-term goals or efforts to expand my mind. And, of course, not realizing that expanding one's mind is really expanding ones "life."

I don't mean to imply that I feel that I have reached some great plateau in my life, but rather I do feel confident, having taken on all the challenges that life has thrown my way, (of which I have created myself) and I feel very optimistic toward my eternal existence. I used to say, as a child, that the happiest day of the year was Christmas because of all the gifts we would receive on Christmas day. However, I later realized that the happiest day was really the day before Christmas when I was very optimistic with "Great Expectations"! (Ah, maybe that's the key to the Charles Dickens' book). Living with that kind of optimism and my knowing that I am ultimately in complete control of my current and future existence, and that I will devour any obstacle that gets in my way, as good food and nourishment for my microcosmic and macrocosmic health and happiness. I have come to realize that *my determination* to fight any obstacle, toward protecting the wellbeing of the universe, is in fact the *infinite lifeforce of the universe*. With that mind, there will always be enough power to overcome anything that trys to stand in my way. If that's not enlightenment it certainly will suffice 'til I get there. And I will get there. I think the most important thing is to discover that true happiness lies nowhere other than within oneself.

I know that so many of us are motivated to achieve that through drugs etc. but one should be aware that rapture is not happiness, and the side effects of many drugs can be devastating in far, far too many cases. I will say that I have had more than my share of drugs, but I've always tried to stay away from those that were addictive, and I rarely even smoke grass anymore, which is legal where I live. At this point in my life, keeping my heart in good health and staying alive is more important. My absolute confidence I have in the causes I am making at the present, to-day, is the source of my ongoing optimism toward the future. It is literally like every day is the day before Christmas. Now, I'm not saying that I don't have obstacles and challenges, which are also a very important part of life. I am saying overcoming obstacles is a confidence builder, and they make you stronger with a way more exciting and interesting life. Can you imagine a movie with no obstacles or challenges? That would be a very dull movie, just as it would be a very dull life. But, to have total confidence that you can overcome any challenges is a great, great, feeling and my optimism for my eternal future soars. That is the best way I can describe where I'm at these days and I can thank the "trauma" I experienced in my life for sending me on this path. There is a Japanese word that is pronounced, "honin myo," which literally means," the mystic nature of the true cause." Or, as we as young American Buddhists use to say, "from this moment on." From this moment on I am determined to spend every moment of my life, every ounce of my energy toward the healthy and happy existence in my home, my community, the world, and this whole infinite thing we call the universe, and every person and thing that is a part of it, until this planet we live on reflects that. That's what we Buddhist call, "kosen rufu" or "world peace". And I hope you will be as determined as I am to do the same.